Hamilton Ontario Book 4 in Colour Photos, Saving Our History One Photo at a Time

Photography
by Barbara Raué
2014

Series Name:
Cruising Ontario

Book 90: Hamilton Book 4

Cover photo: 105 Aberdeen Avenue

Series Name: Cruising Ontario
Saving Our History One Photo at a Time
in colour photos

Other Books by Barbara Raue

Coins of Gold

Arrows, Indians and Love

The Life and Times of Barbara
Volume 1: Inventions That Have Enhanced My Life
Volume 2: Entertainment That I Have Enjoyed
Volume 3: East Coast Trips
Volume 4: Olympics Have Always Intrigued Me
Volume 5: Wonders of the World
Volume 6: Caribbean Cruises We Have Enjoyed
Volume 7: Animals
Volume 8: Storms and Other Major Disasters in My Lifetime
Volume 9: Wars, Terrorist Attacks and Major Disasters

The Cromwell Family Book

Laura Secord Discovered

Visit Barbara's website to view all of her books
http://barbararaue.ca

In 1784, thousands of United Empire Loyalists settled in Upper Canada (what is now southern Ontario). They were soon followed by more Americans attracted by the availability of inexpensive, arable land. Large numbers of Iroquois loyal to Britain arrived from the United States and were settled on reserves. Between 1788 and 1793, the townships at the Head-of-the-Lake were surveyed and named.

Hamilton, the centre of a densely populated and industrialized region, is located in Southern Ontario on the western part of Lake Ontario. There are over one hundred waterfalls and cascades within the city, most of which are on or near the Bruce Trail as it winds through the Niagara Escarpment.

Two steel manufacturing companies, Stelco and Dofasco, were formed in 1910 and 1912, and Procter & Gamble opened a manufacturing plant in 1914. The Pigott Building was the city's first high-rise building constructed in 1929. McMaster University moved from Toronto to Hamilton, an airport was built in 1940, a Studebaker assembly line started in 1948, the Burlington Bay Skyway Bridge was built in 1958, and the first Tim Horton's store opened in 1964.

Hamilton is home to the Royal Botanical Gardens, McMaster University and Mohawk College. The Canadian Football League's Hamilton Tiger Cats began playing at the new Tim Hortons Field in 2014, which was built as part of the 2015 Pan American Games which will be jointly hosted by Toronto and Hamilton.

On January 1, 2001, the new City of Hamilton was formed through the amalgamation of the former city and six surrounding municipalities. We have lived in Hamilton for more than 40 years; it is here that we raised our three children.

Table of Contents

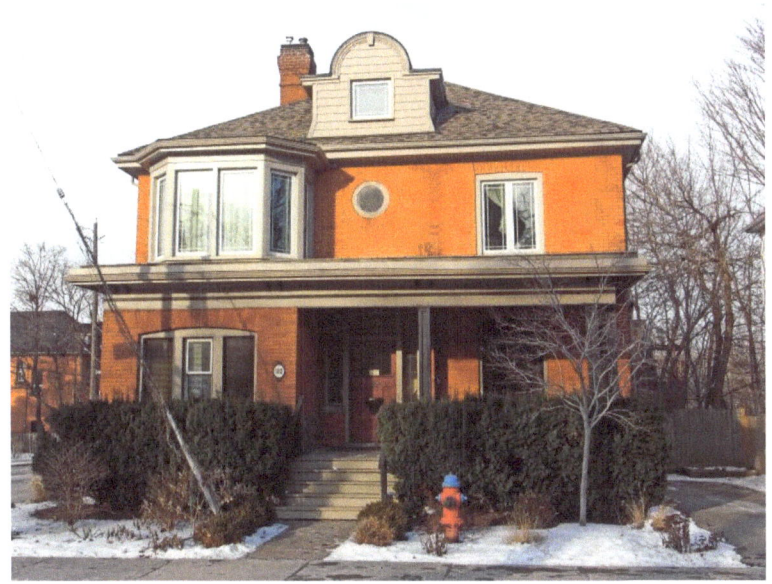

182 Aberdeen Avenue – Italianate, dormer, bay window

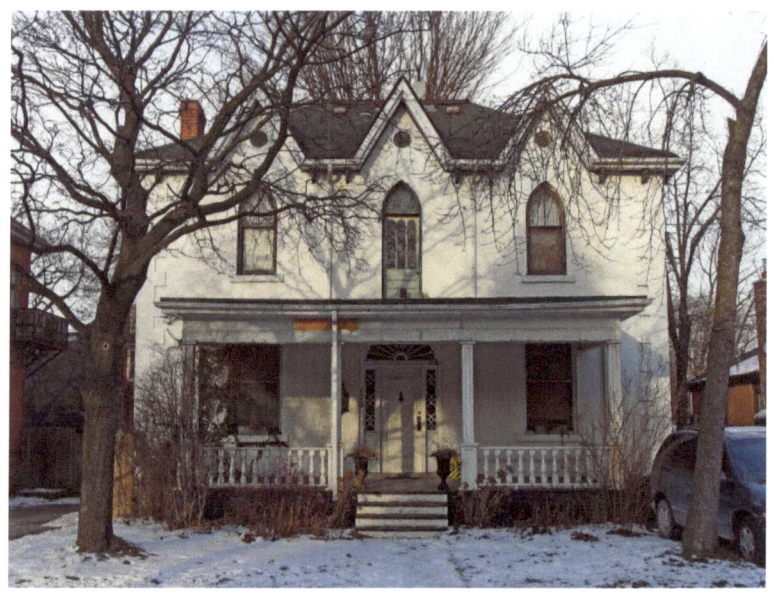

178 Aberdeen Avenue – triple arch Gothic Revival

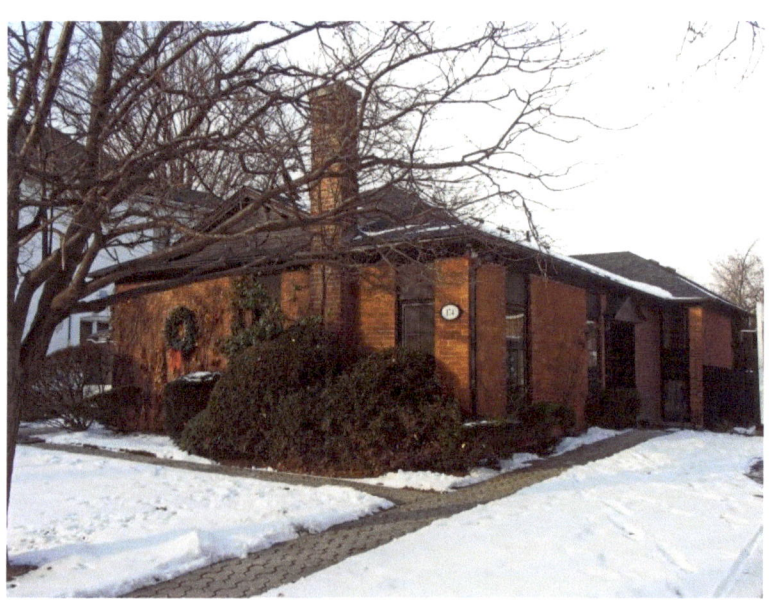

174 Aberdeen Avenue – Regency Cottage

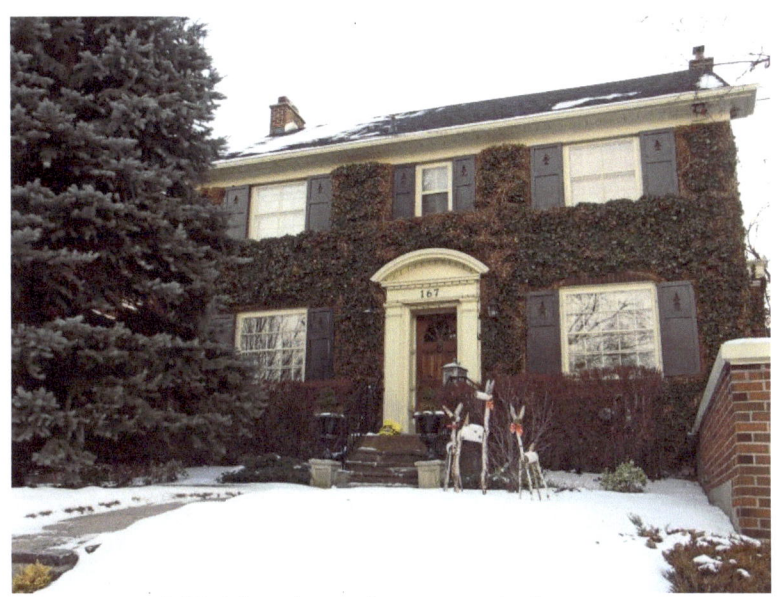

167 Aberdeen Avenue - Italianate

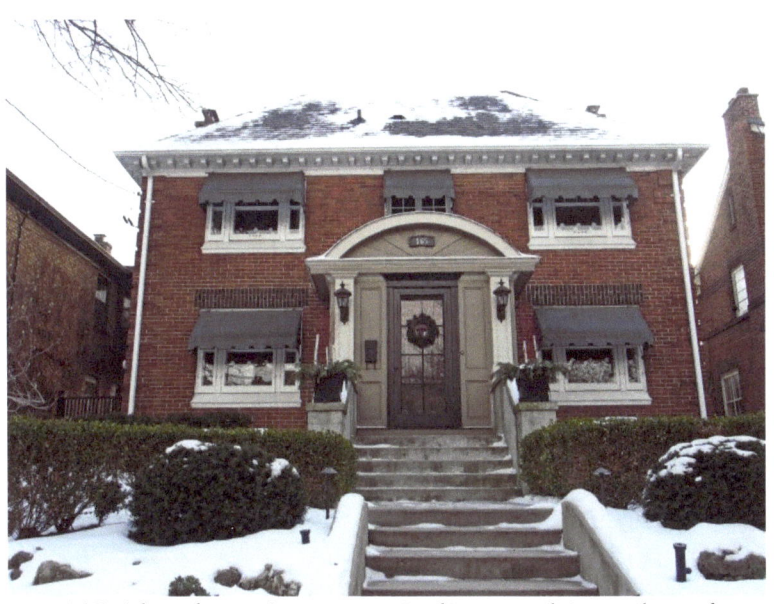

165 Aberdeen Avenue – Italianate, hipped roof

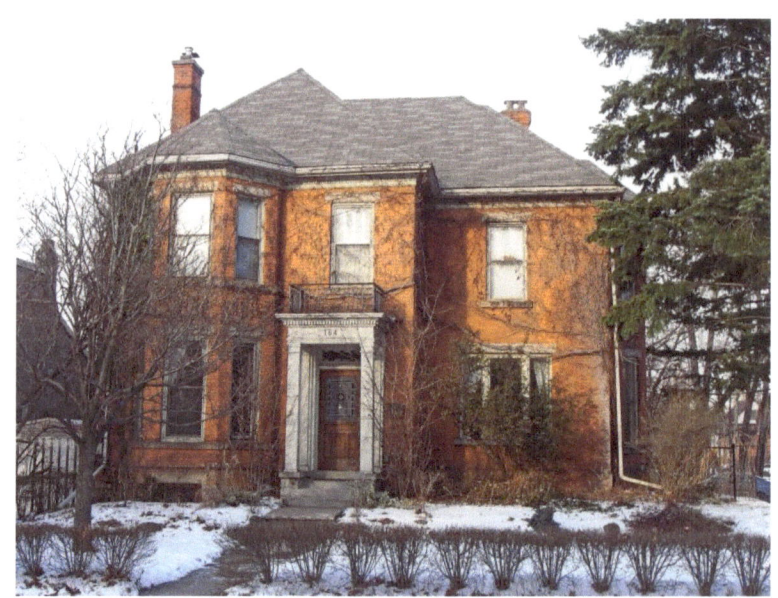

164 Aberdeen Avenue – Italianate, hipped roof, two-storey bay window

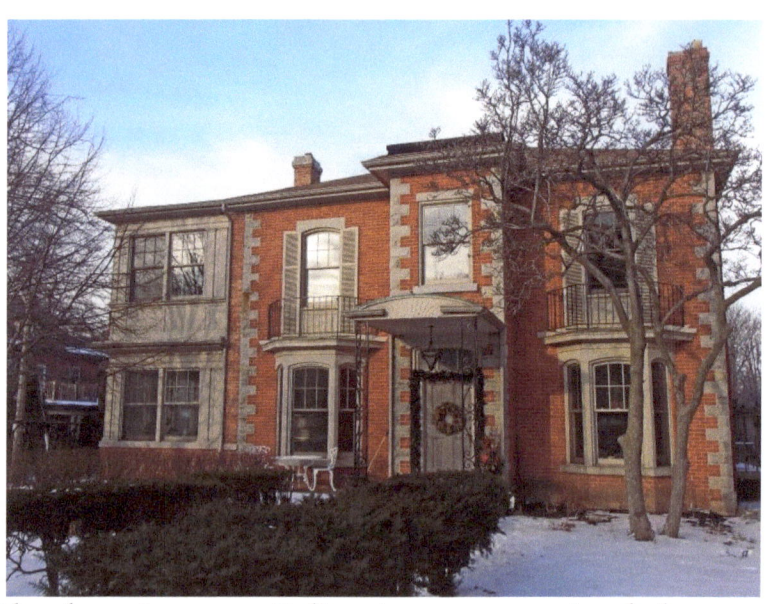

Aberdeen Avenue – Italianate, corner quoins, balcony on second floor above bay window

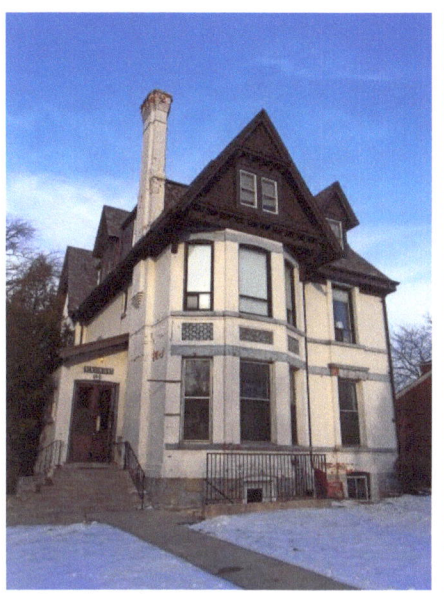

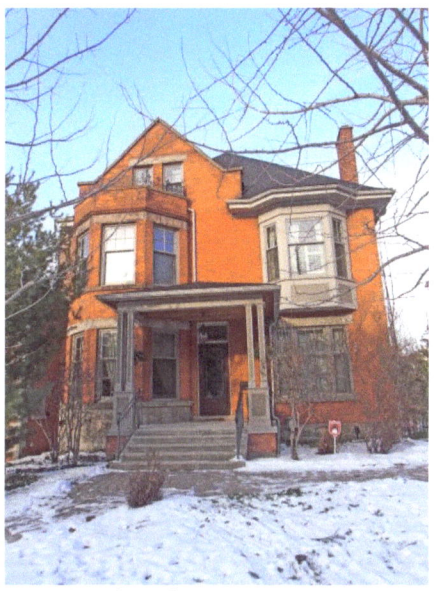

160 Aberdeen Avenue
(corner of Hess) - Gothic

148 Aberdeen Avenue

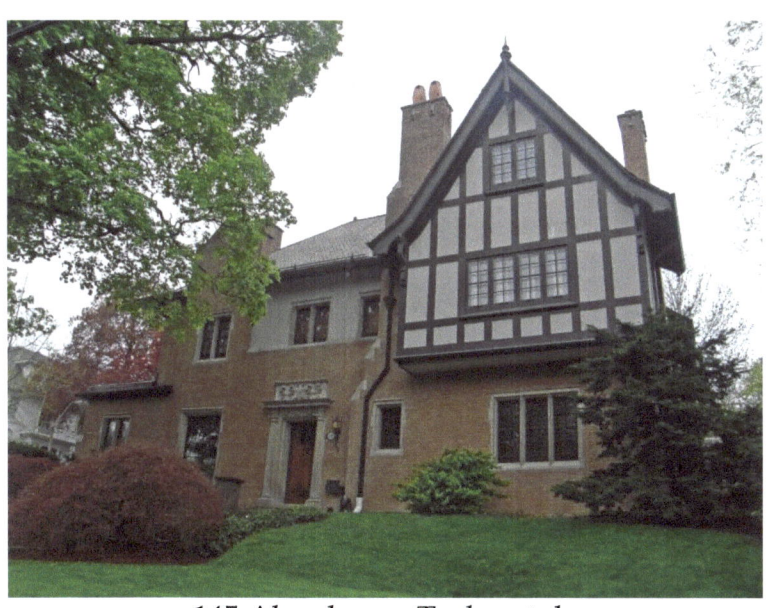

145 Aberdeen – Tudor style

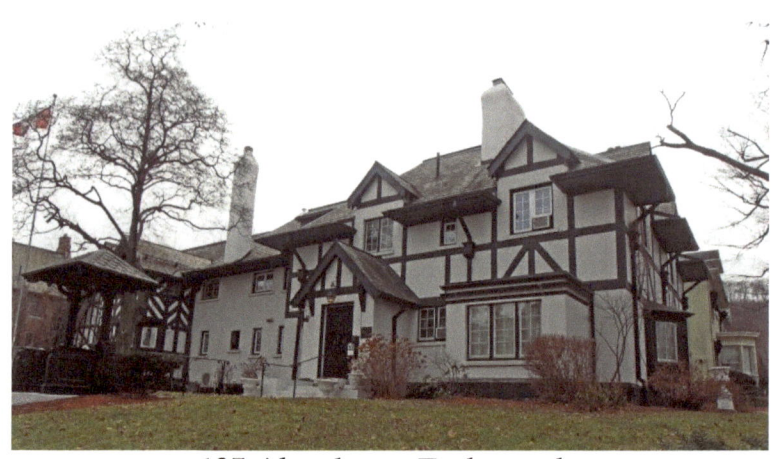

135 Aberdeen - Tudor style

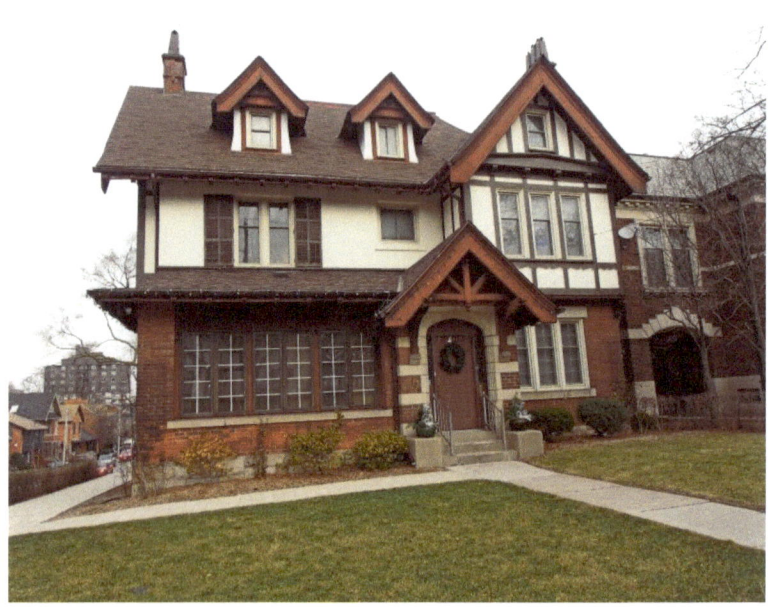

126 Aberdeen Avenue – Tudor style, dormers

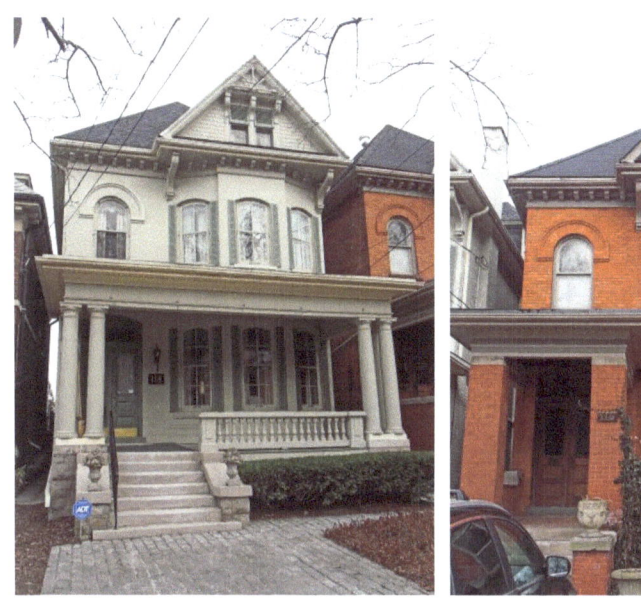

118 Aberdeen Avenue   115 Aberdeen Avenue
Edwardian style, Romanesque style window arches,
bay windows

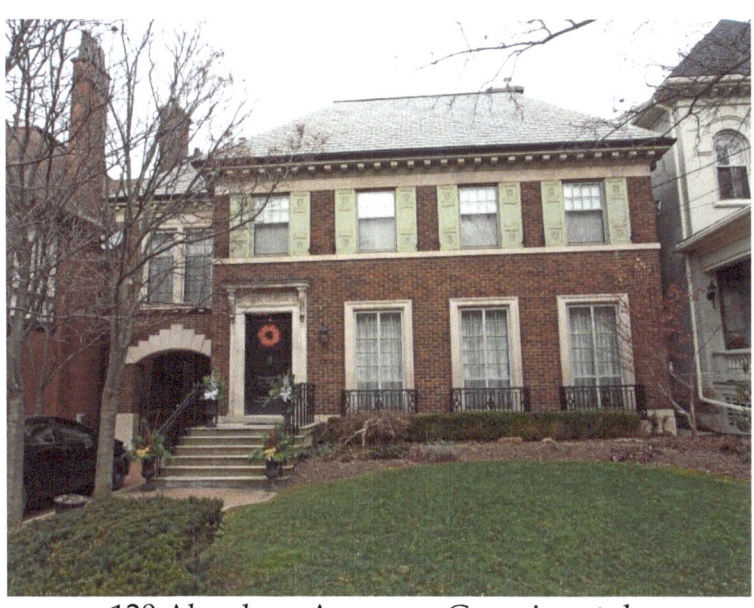

120 Aberdeen Avenue – Georgian style

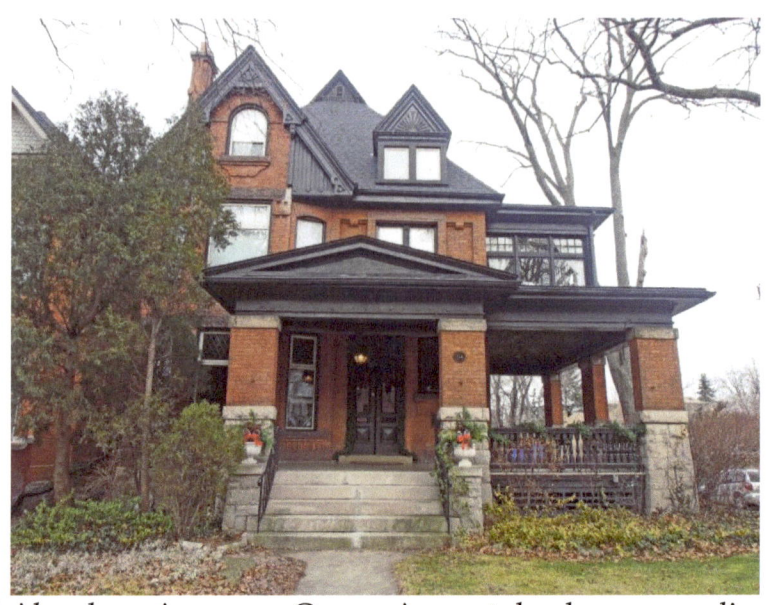

114 Aberdeen Avenue – Queen Anne style, dormer, pediment, wraparound verandah

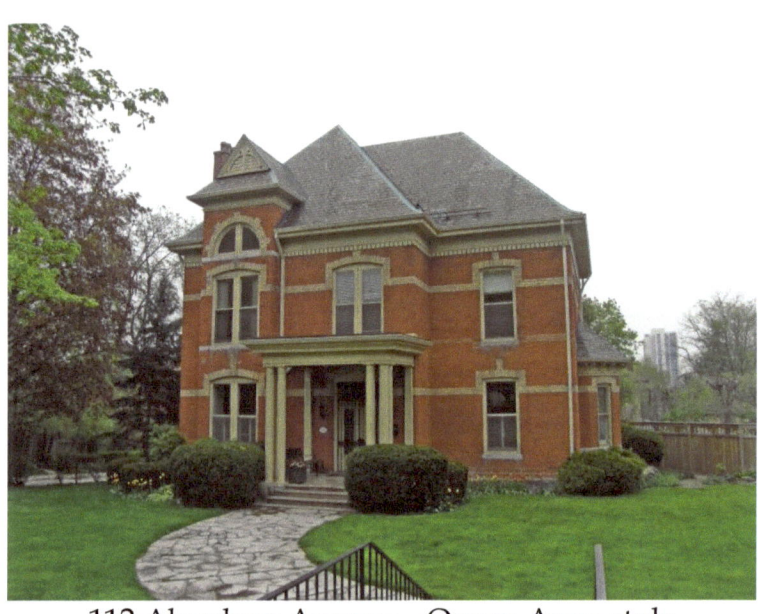

112 Aberdeen Avenue – Queen Anne style

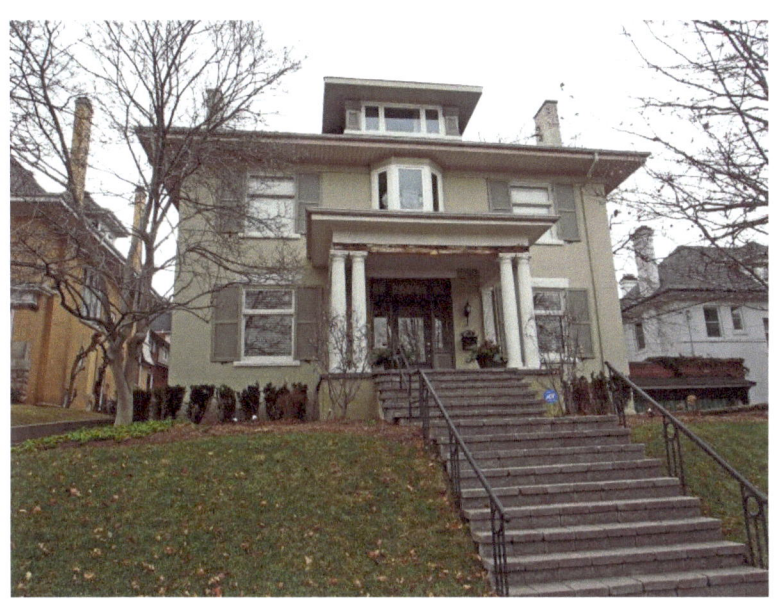

109 Aberdeen Avenue – Italianate style, dormer

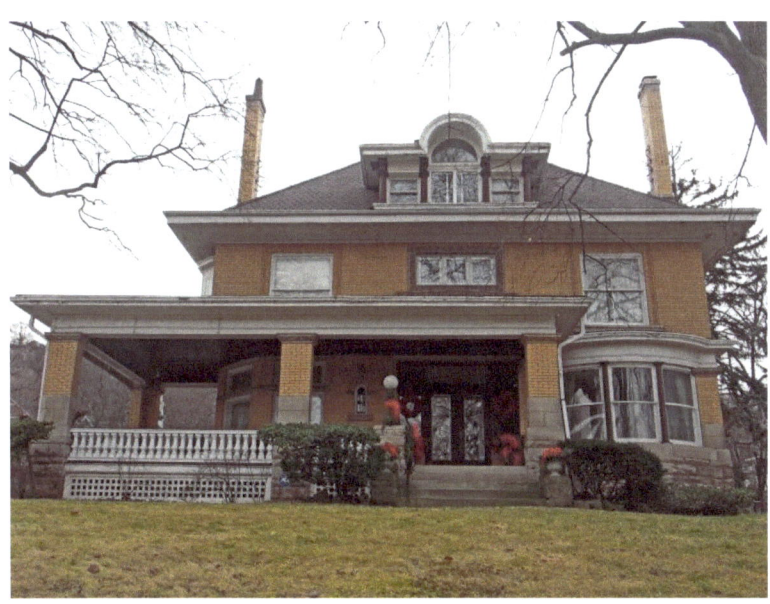

107 Aberdeen Avenue – Haddo House built 1908
Italianate, ornate dormer, wraparound verandah, bay window

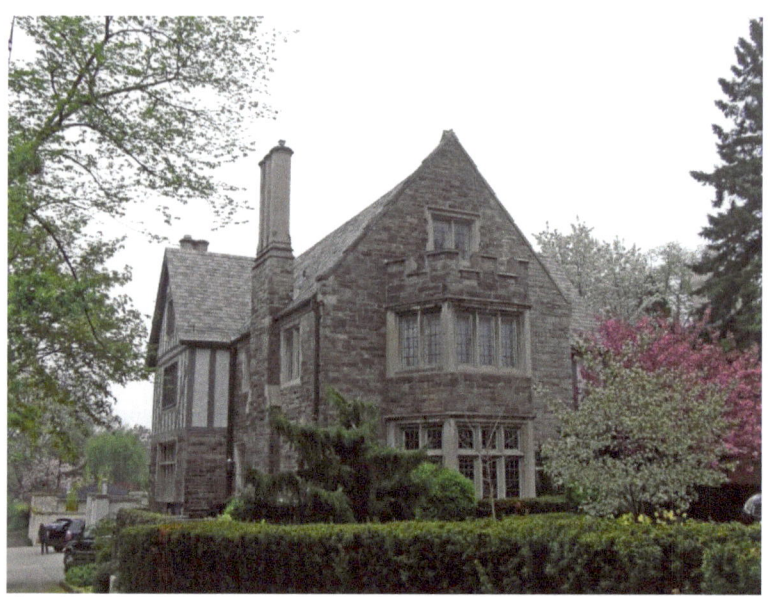

108 Aberdeen Avenue "Burnewin" – built 1932 - designed by architect William Souter as his own residence. It is made of stone. Originally, Souter intended to purchase the house immediately to the east, tear it down, and convert its lot into his front garden entrance on Bay Street South. It's for this reason the front door of the house faces east and not onto Aberdeen Avenue.

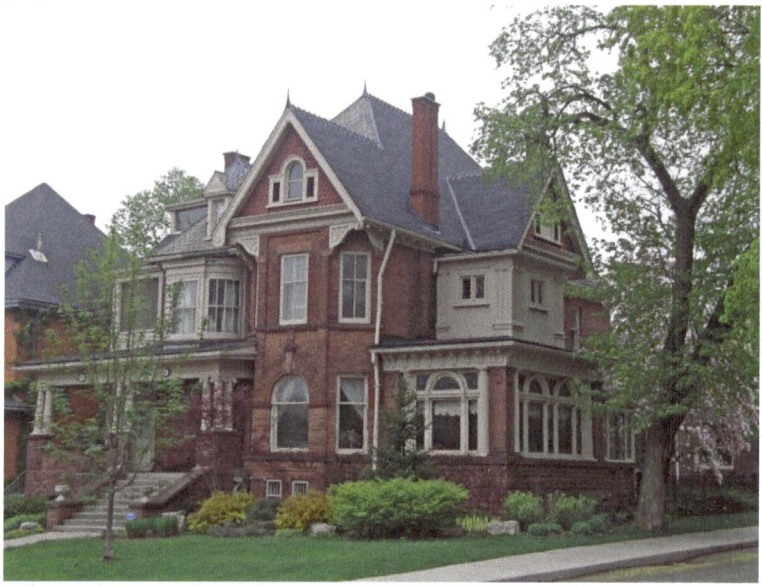

Edwardian style, Palladian window, fretwork, bay window

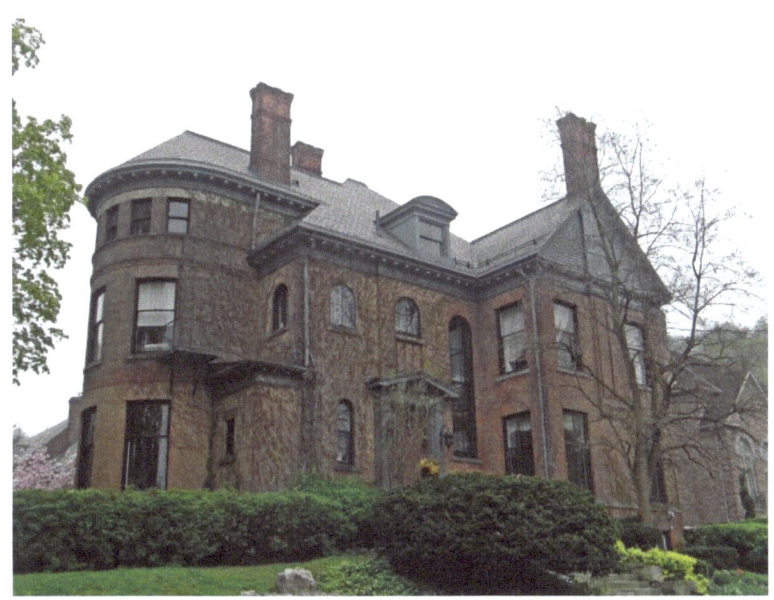

105 Aberdeen Avenue – built in 1893 in the Queen Anne style

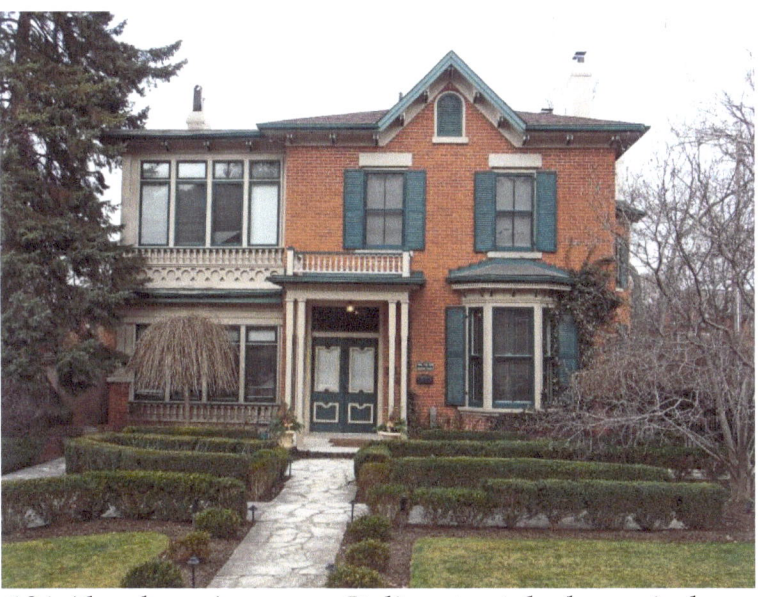

104 Aberdeen Avenue – Italianate style, bay window, cornice brackets

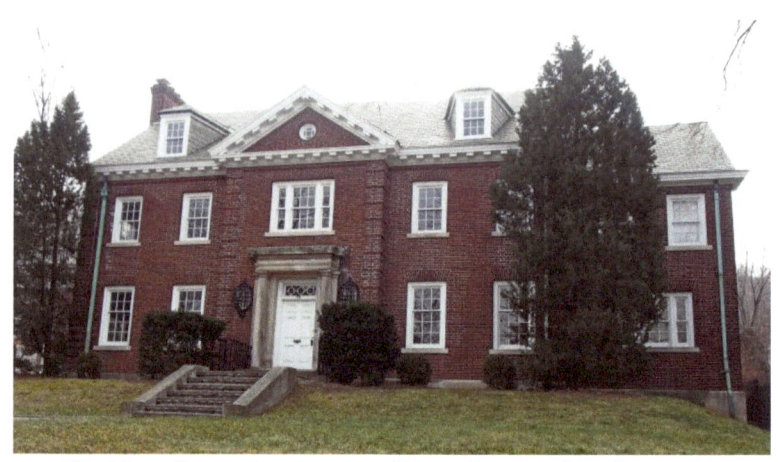

73 Aberdeen Avenue – Georgian style, dormers

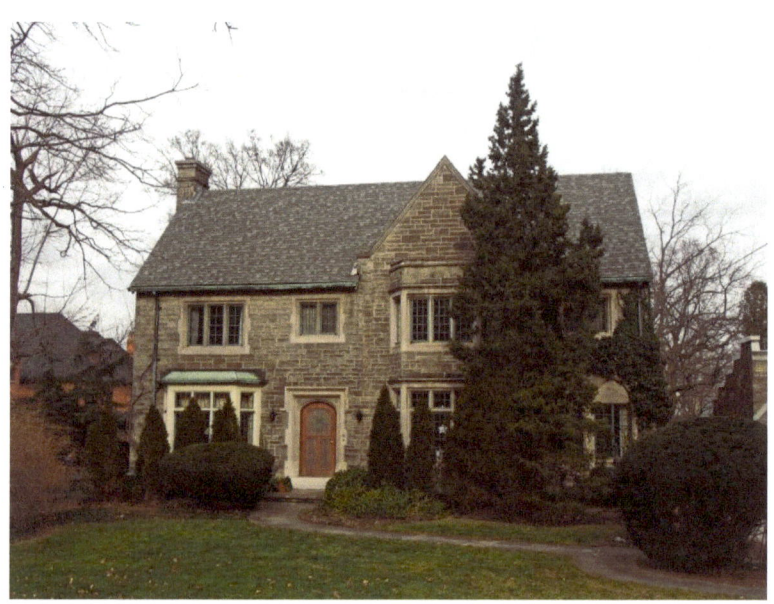

70 Aberdeen Avenue - stone

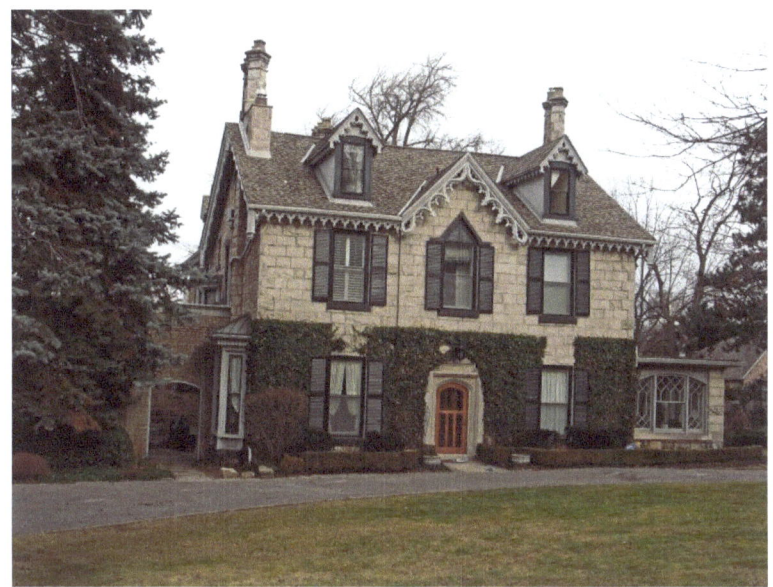

64 Aberdeen Avenue – made of cut stone in Gothic Revival style – 1892 - gingerbread bargeboard, dormers

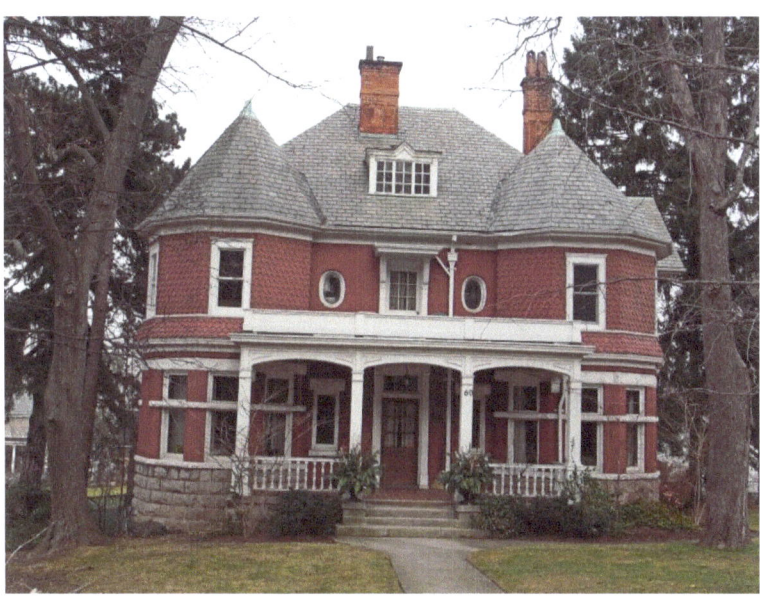

60 Aberdeen Avenue – built 1899 – Queen Anne style, turrets

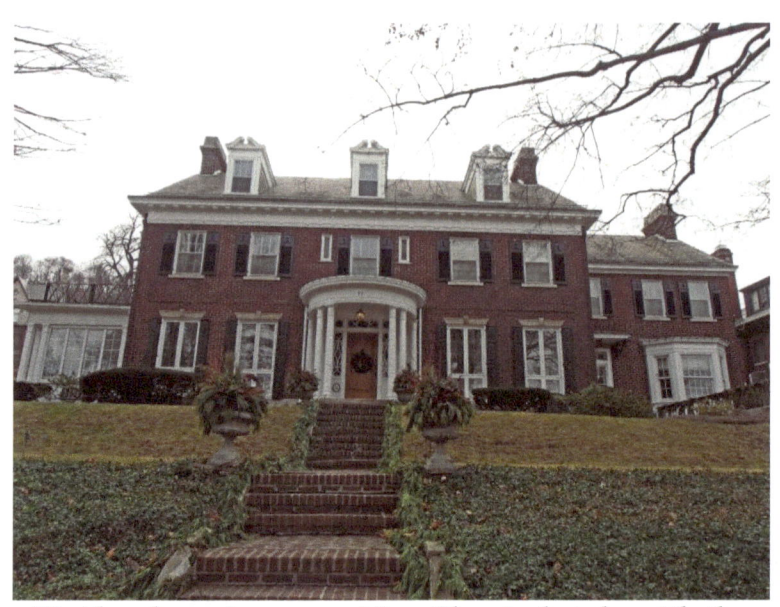

51 Aberdeen Avenue – Neo-Classical style with the colonnaded half-round portico, dormers

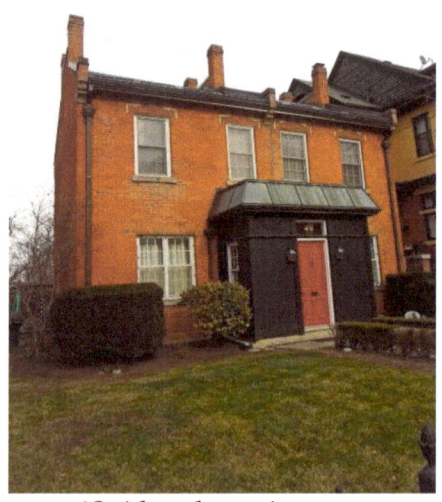

48 Aberdeen Avenue

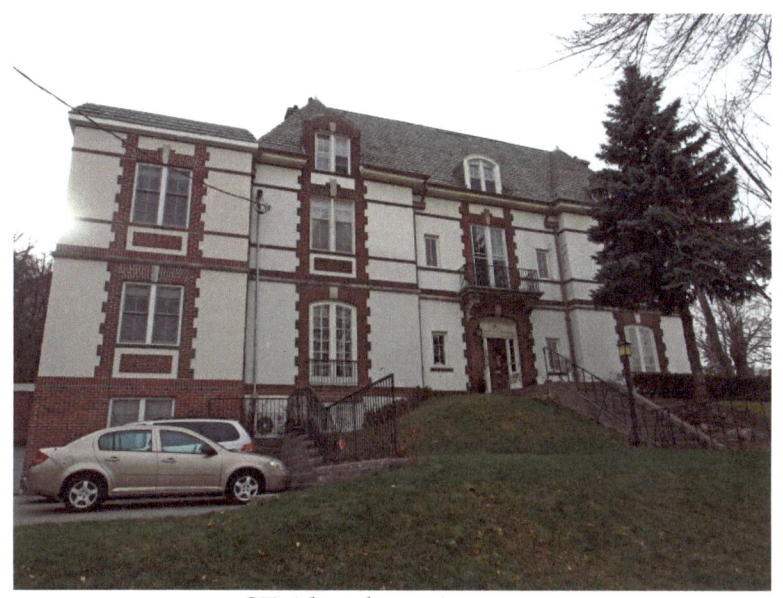

37 Aberdeen Avenue

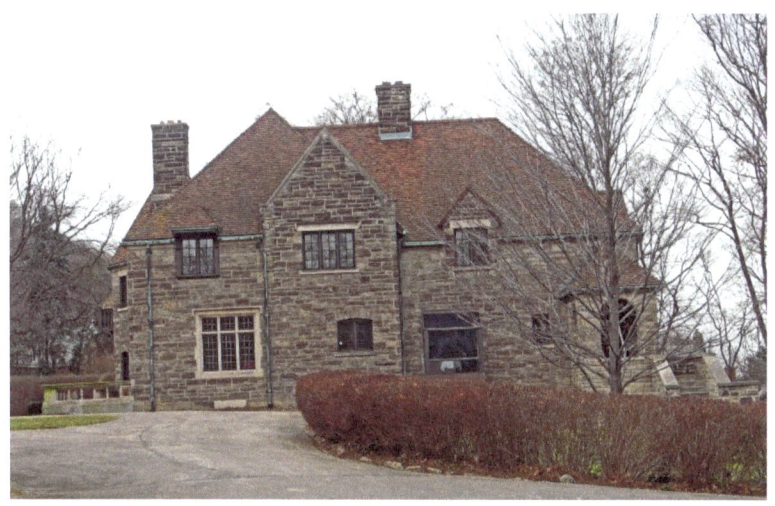

362 Bay Street South - Built in 1933 in the style of a Norman manor house seen in France – reinforced concrete and concrete block with a cut stone cladding

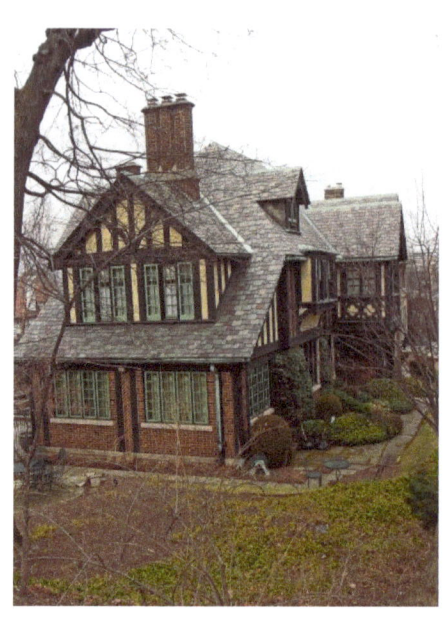

358 Bay Street South - Tudor Revival style

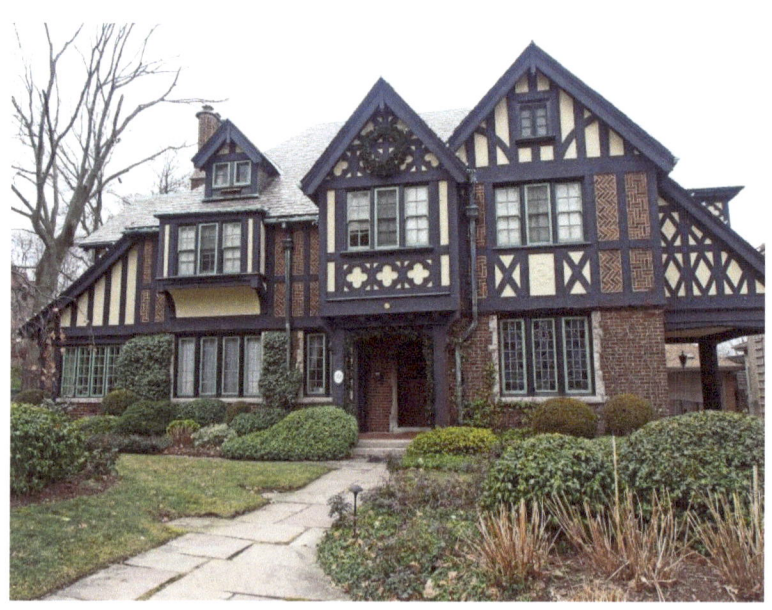

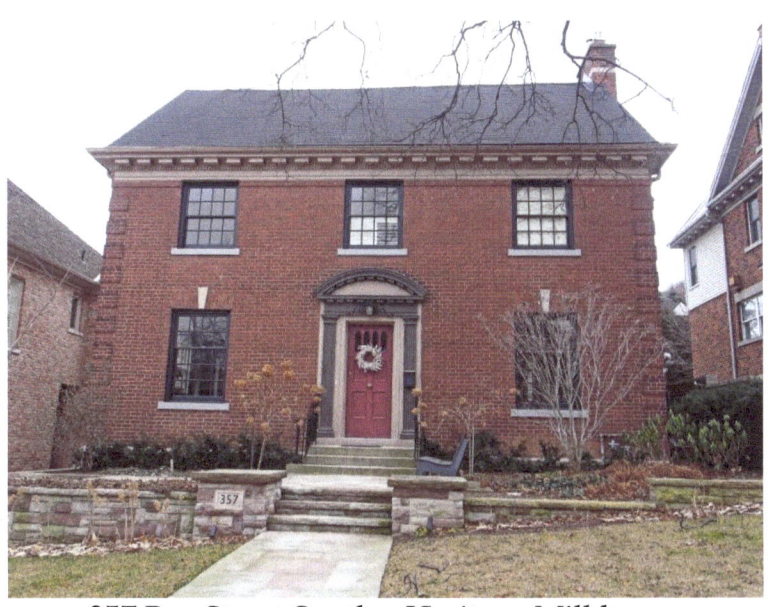

357 Bay Street South – Heritage Mill house
Italianate, dentil moulding

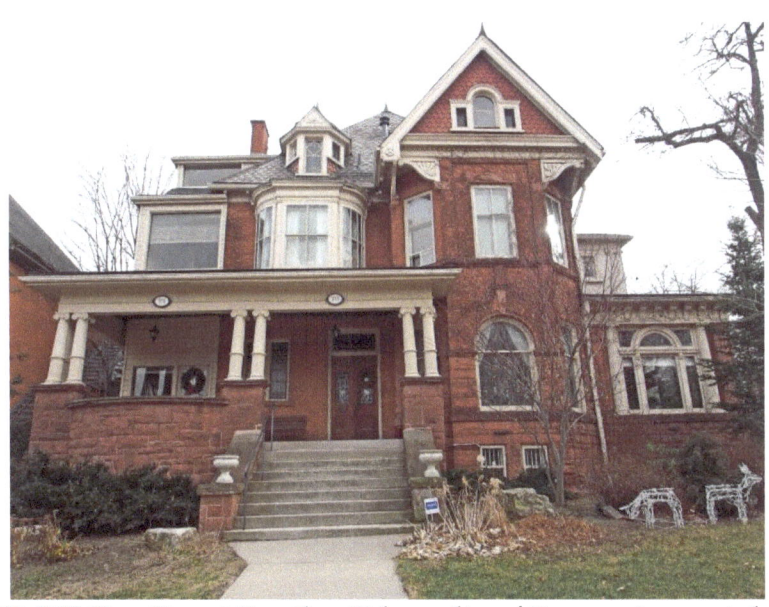

351-353 Bay Street South – Edwardian/Queen Anne styles,
Palladian window, Ionic capitals on verandah pillars,
bay window, dormer

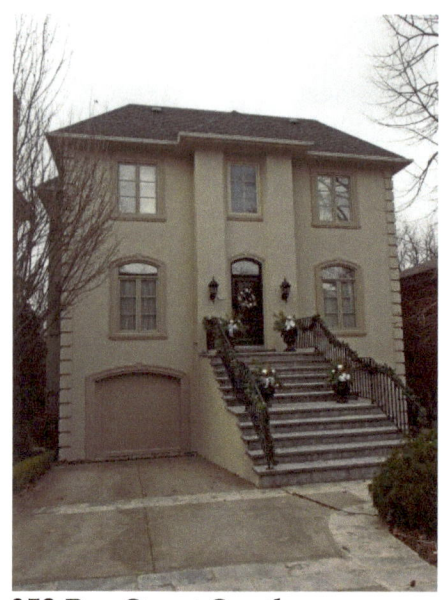
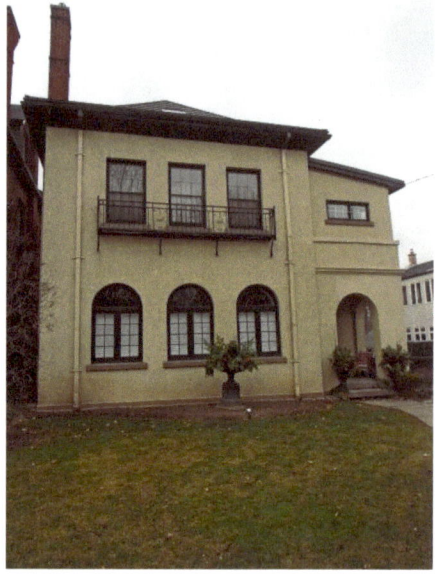

352 Bay Street South

Bay Street South

Italianate, hipped roofs

Corner quoins

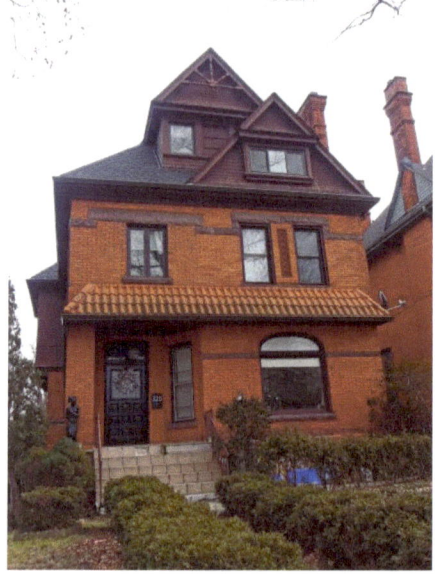
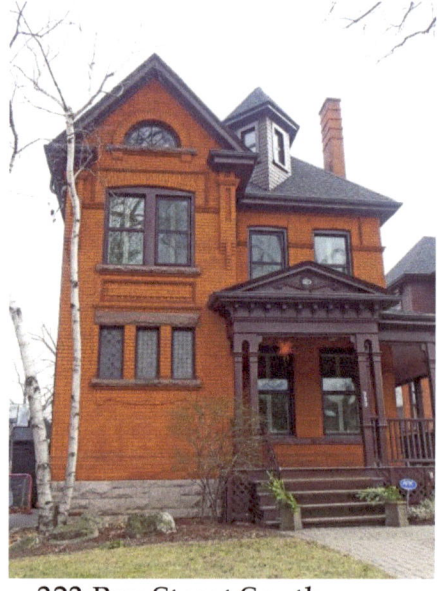

325 Bay Street South
Italianate, dormers

323 Bay Street South
Edwardian, pediment,
dormer, cornice return on gable

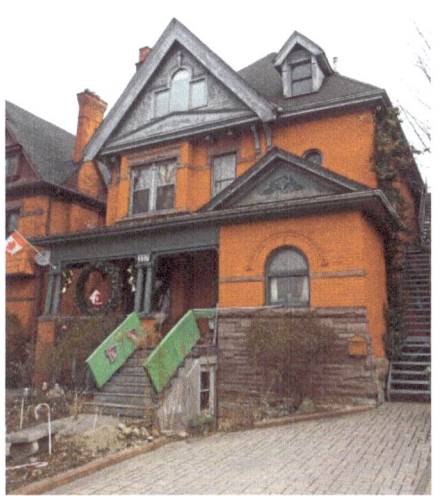

327 Bay Street South – Edwardian, Palladian window, dormer, pediment

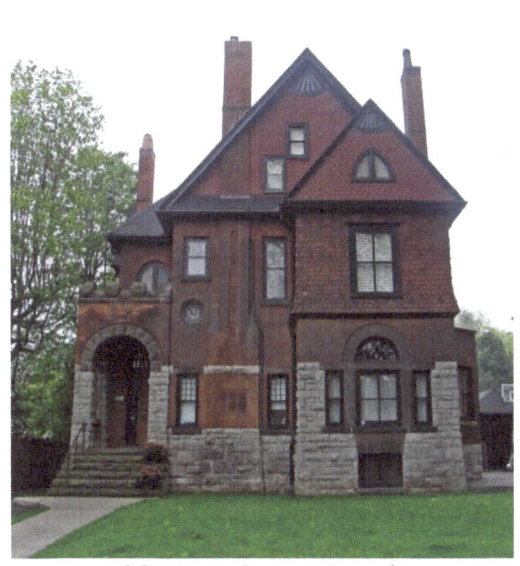

321 Bay Street South

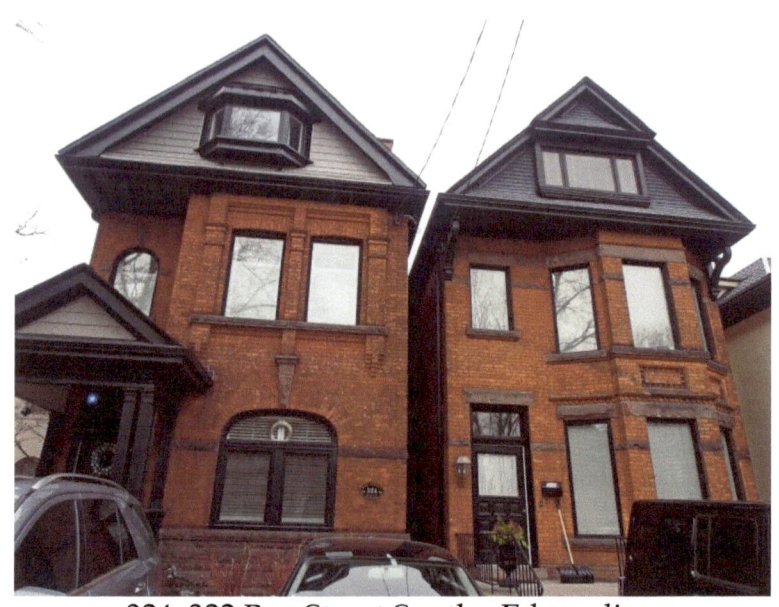

324, 322 Bay Street South - Edwardian

Pediment   two-storey bay window

Arched voussoir, keystone

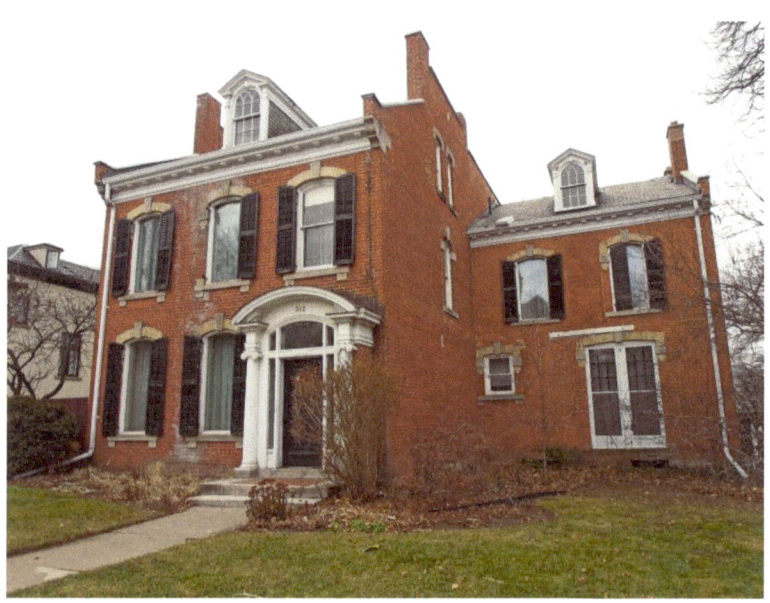

312 Bay Street – Italianate, dormers

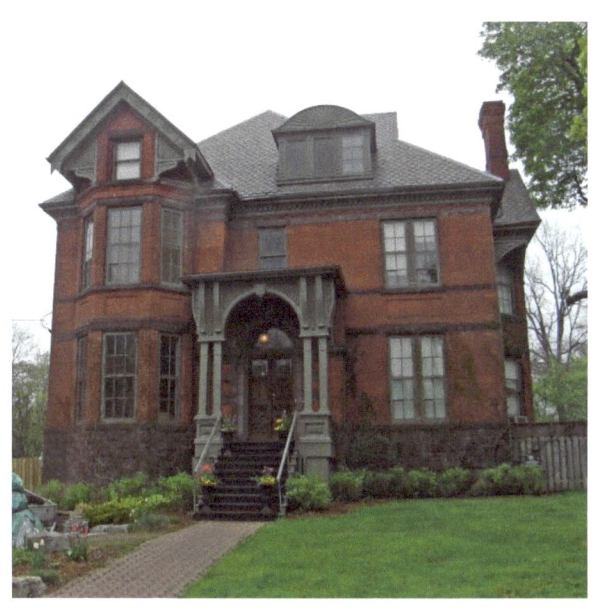

311 Bay Street – Edwardian/Queen Anne, fretwork

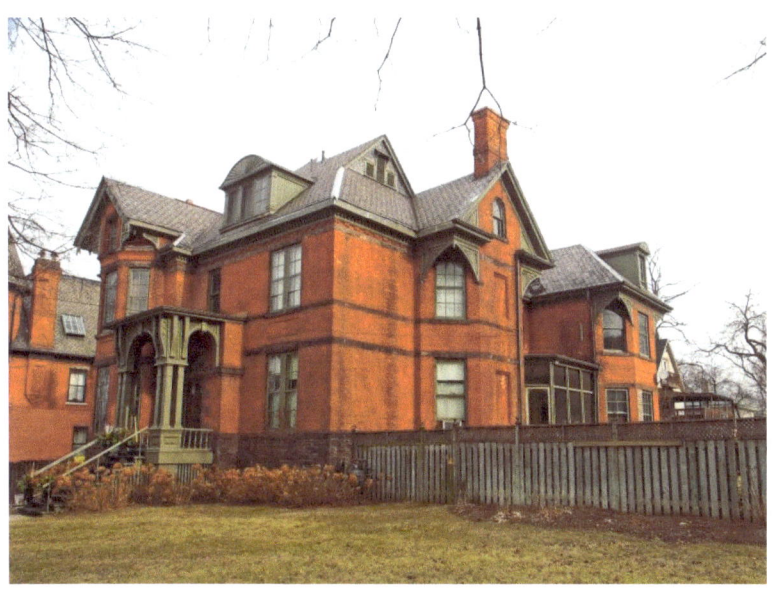

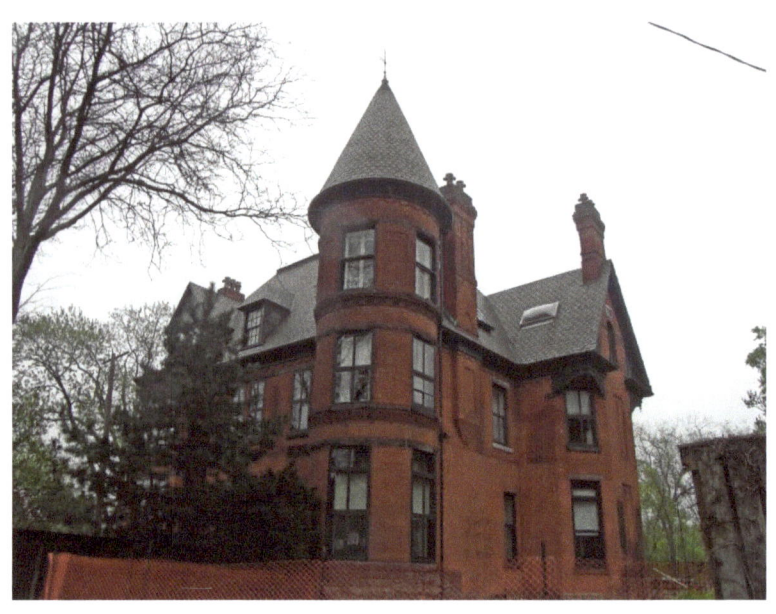

301 Bay Street South (corner of Markland) – Queen Anne style, built 1890, three-storey turret

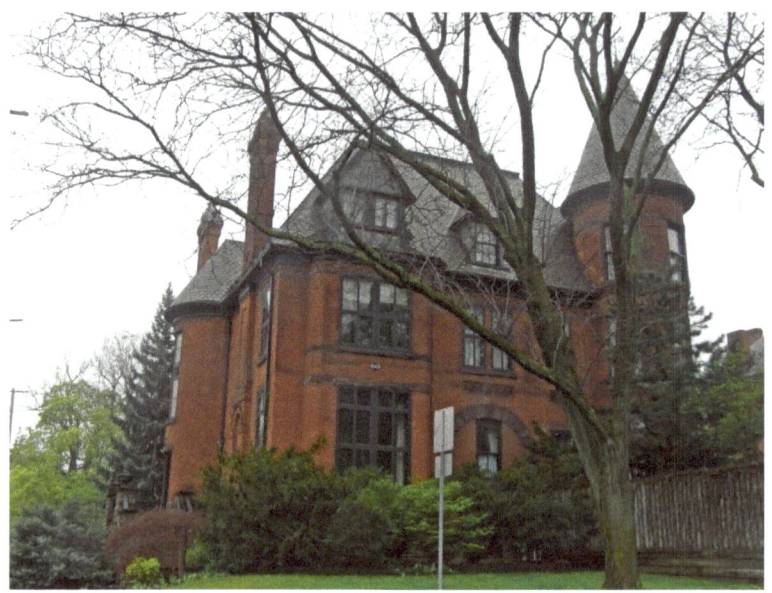

301 Bay Street

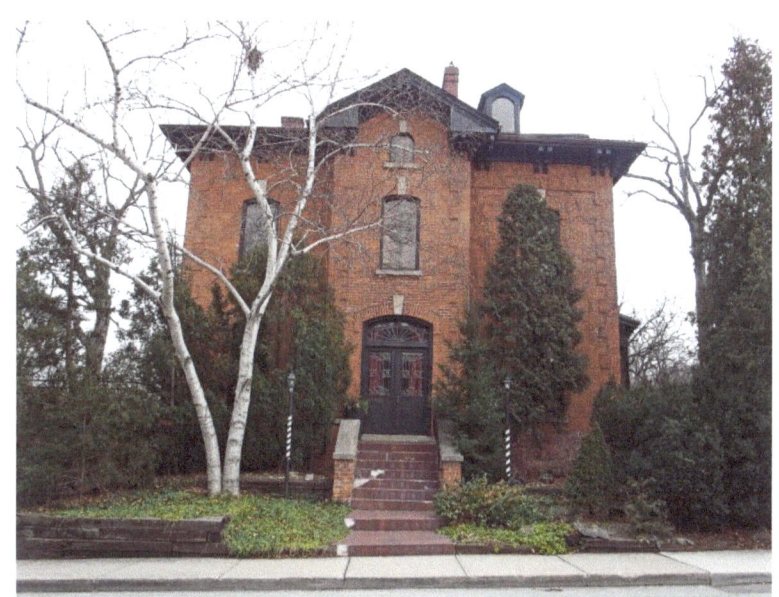

295 Bay Street South – cornice brackets,
two-and-a-half storey frontispiece, dormer

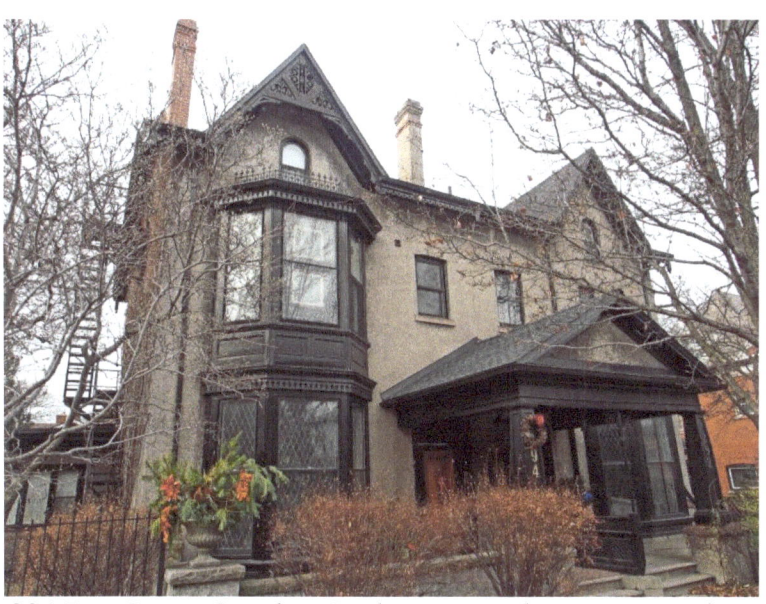

294 Bay Street South – Gothic Revival, two-storey bay
window, iron cresting, verge board trim, pediment

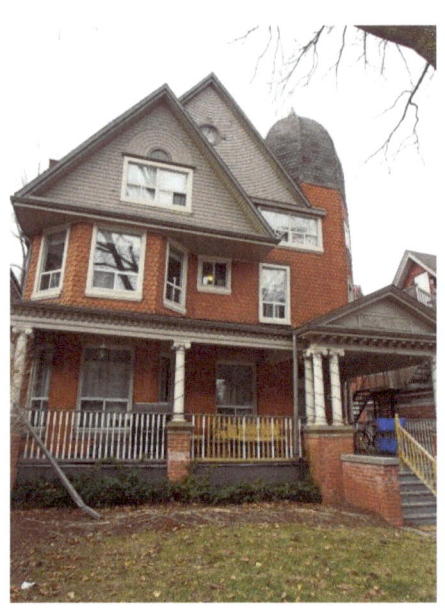

280 Bay Street South – "Bright Side" - Queen Anne style, turret, Ionic capitals on verandah pillars, pediment

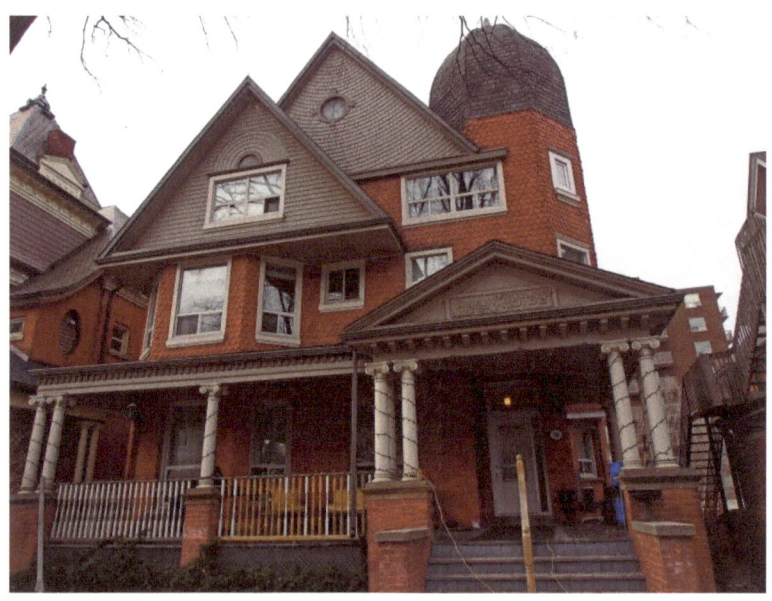

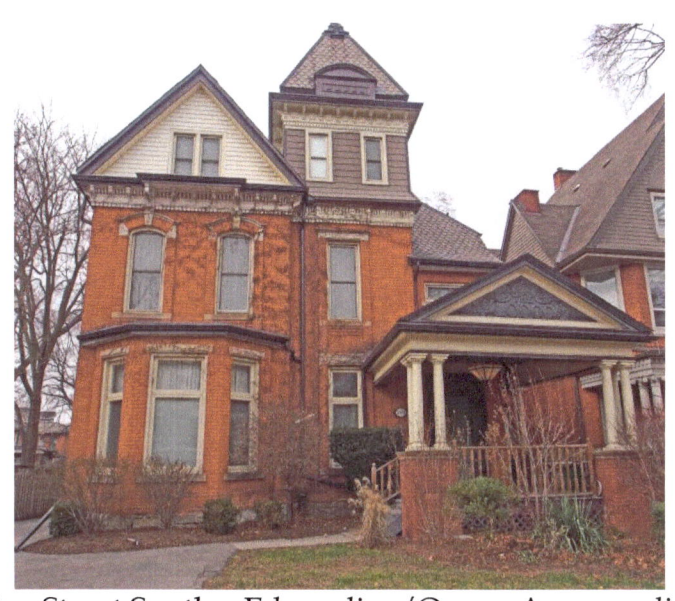

282 Bay Street South – Edwardian/Queen Anne, pediment, bay window - "The Lodge"

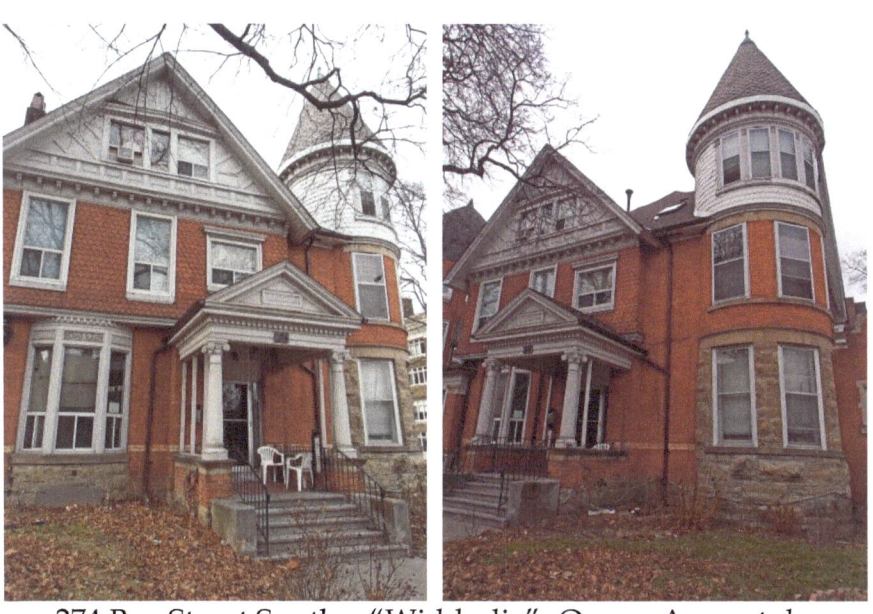

274 Bay Street South – "Widderlie"- Queen Anne style, three-storey turret, pediment above porch with Ionic capitals on pillars

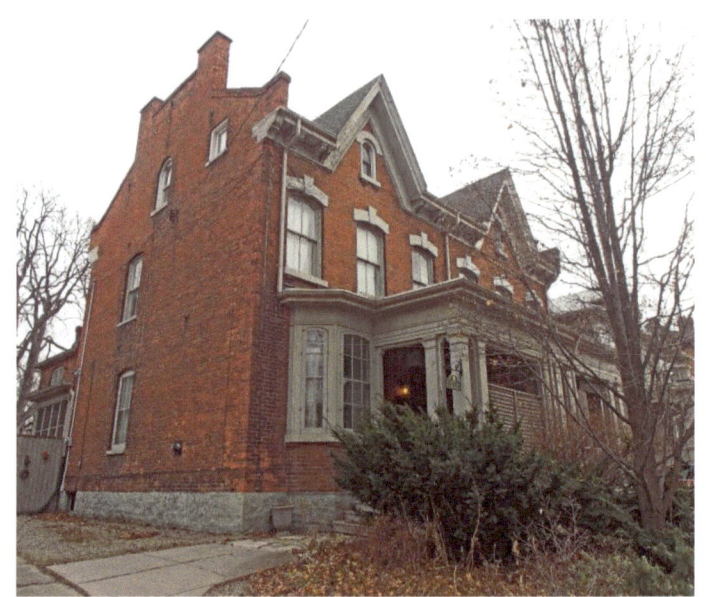

279 Bay street South – Gothic Revival

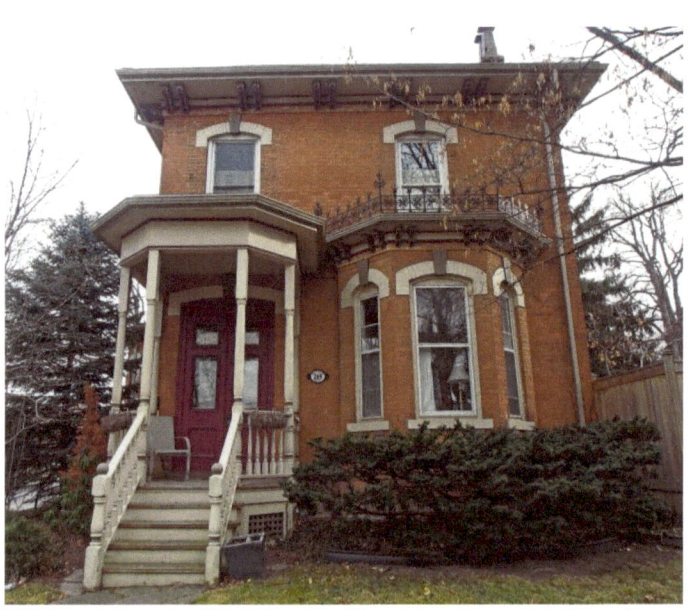

269 Bay Street South – Italianate, cornice brackets, bay window with iron cresting above

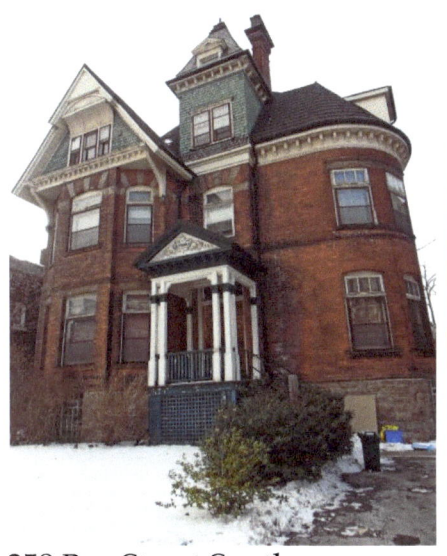 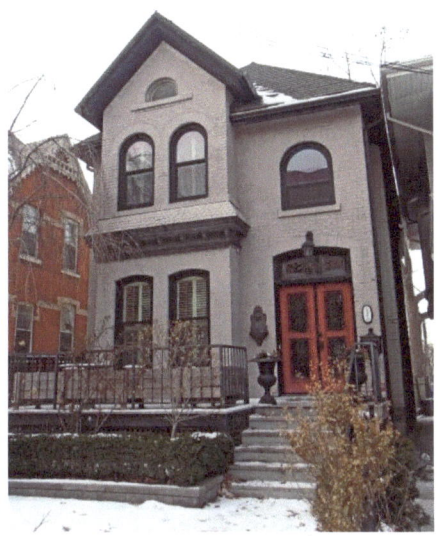

258 Bay Street South
Queen Anne style
Pediment above entrance

230 Bay Street South

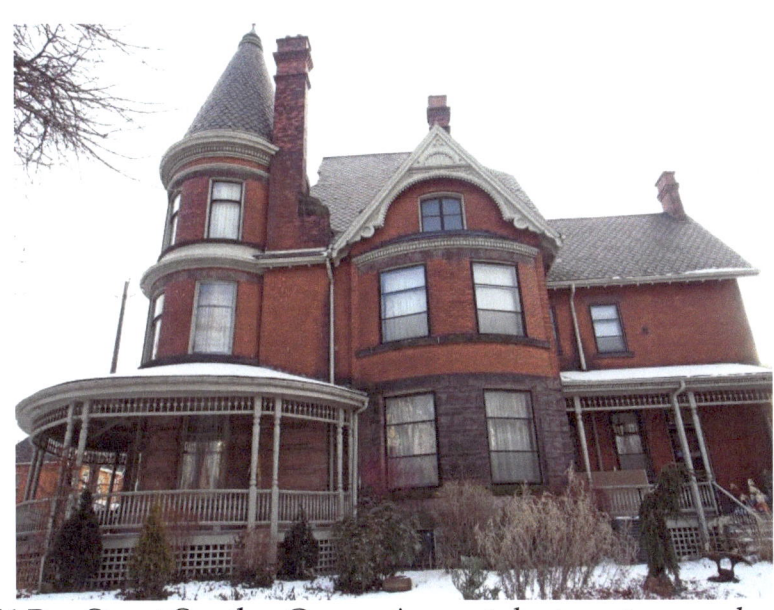

254 Bay Street South – Queen Anne style, turret, verge board trim on gable, wraparound verandah

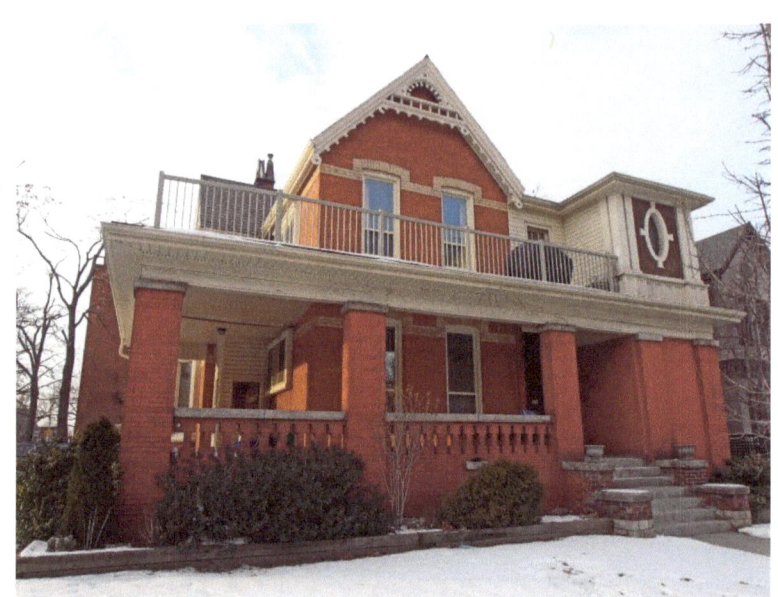

234 Bay Street South – Gothic Revival, verge board trim on gable, second floor verandah

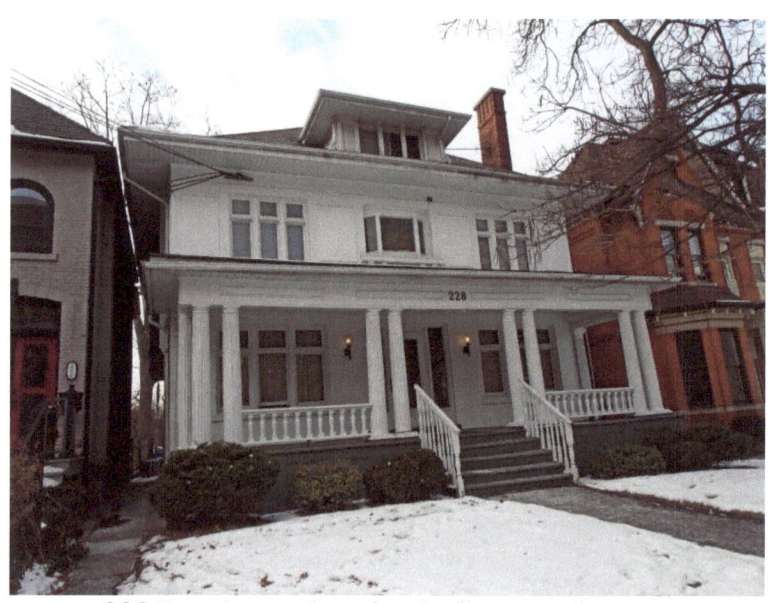

228 Bay Street South – Italianate, dormer

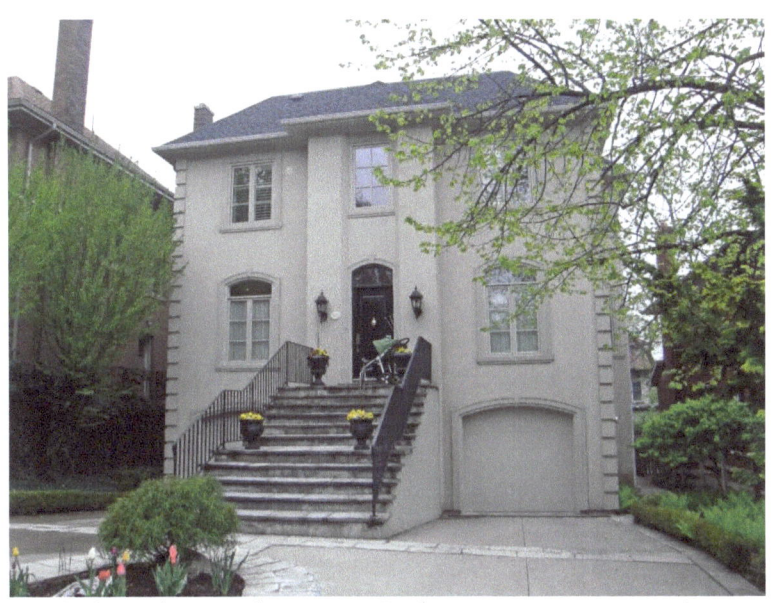

352 Inglewood Drive – Italianate, corner quoins

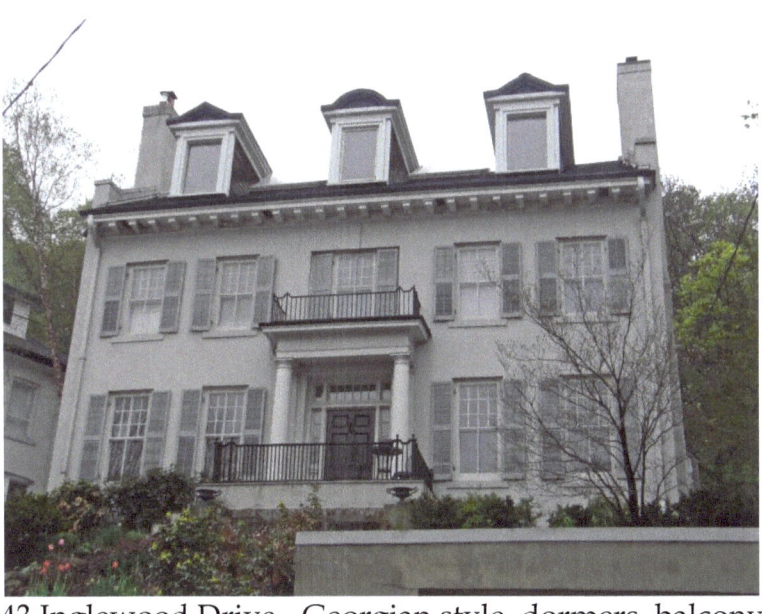

43 Inglewood Drive - Georgian style, dormers, balcony

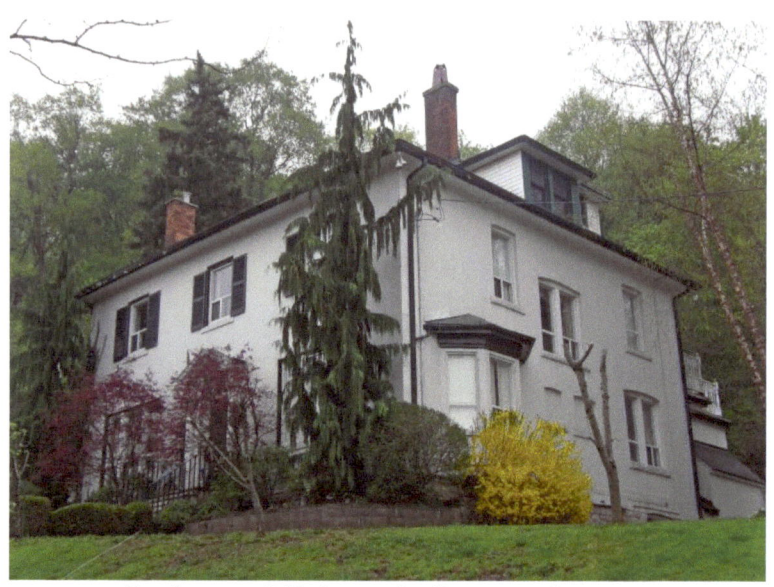

Inglewood Drive – Italianate, dormer

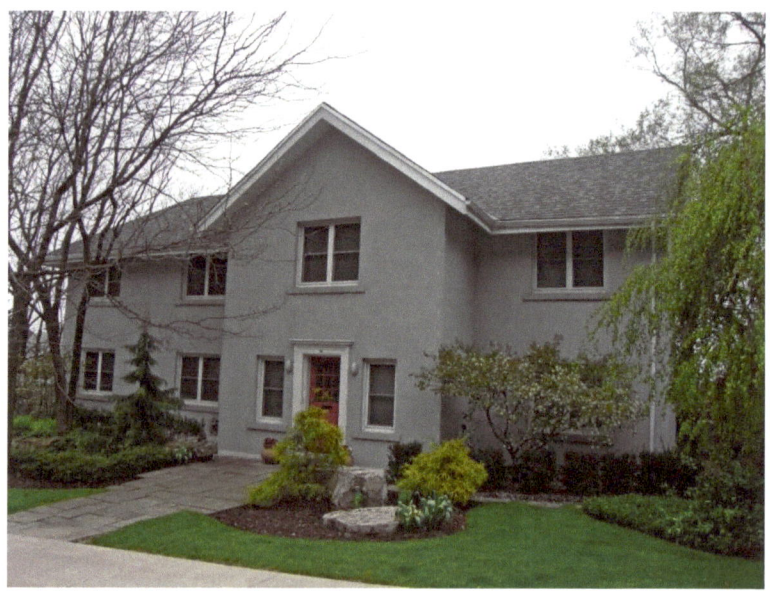

44 Inglewood Drive

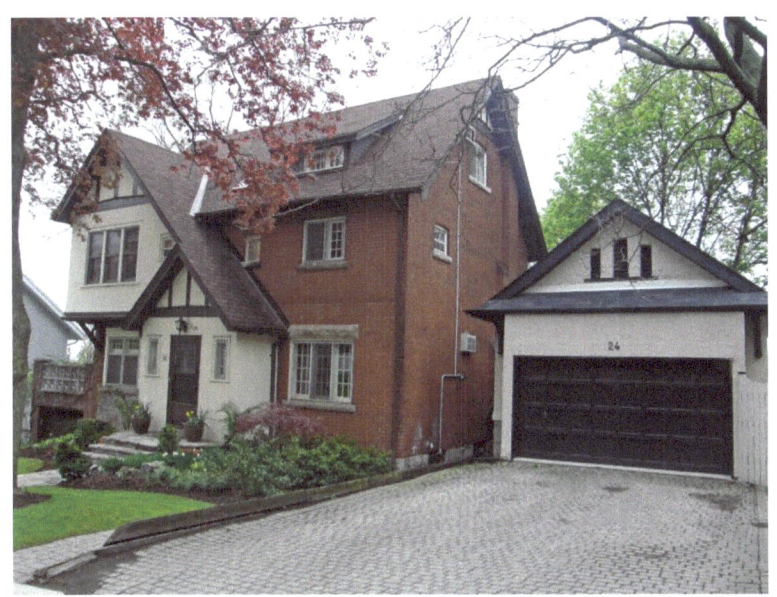

30 Inglewood Drive

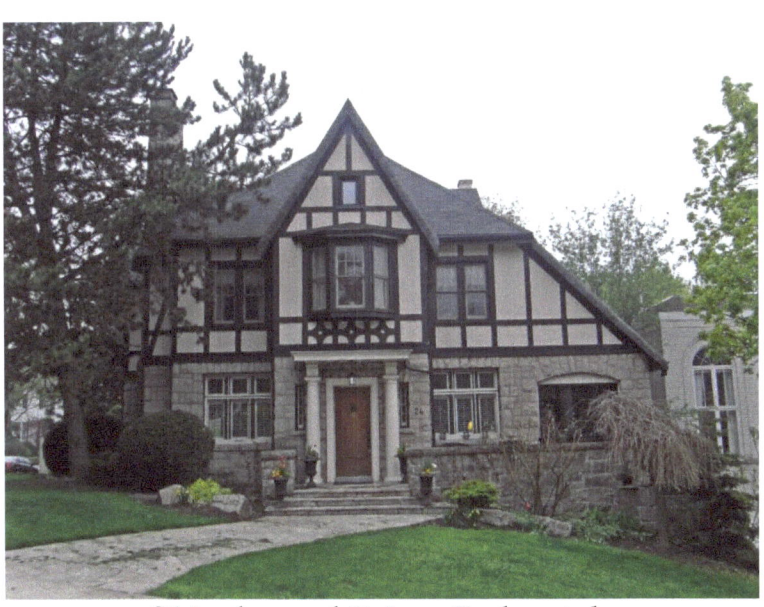

24 Inglewood Drive - Tudor style

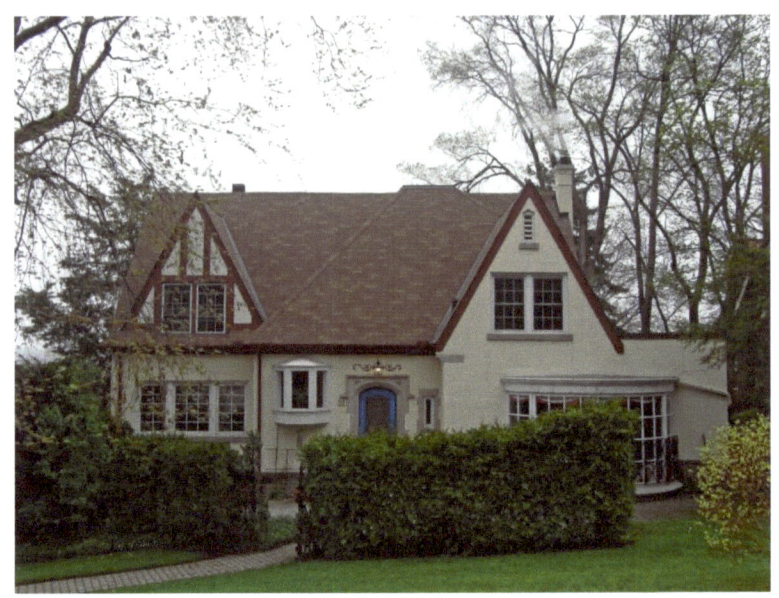

22 Inglewood Drive

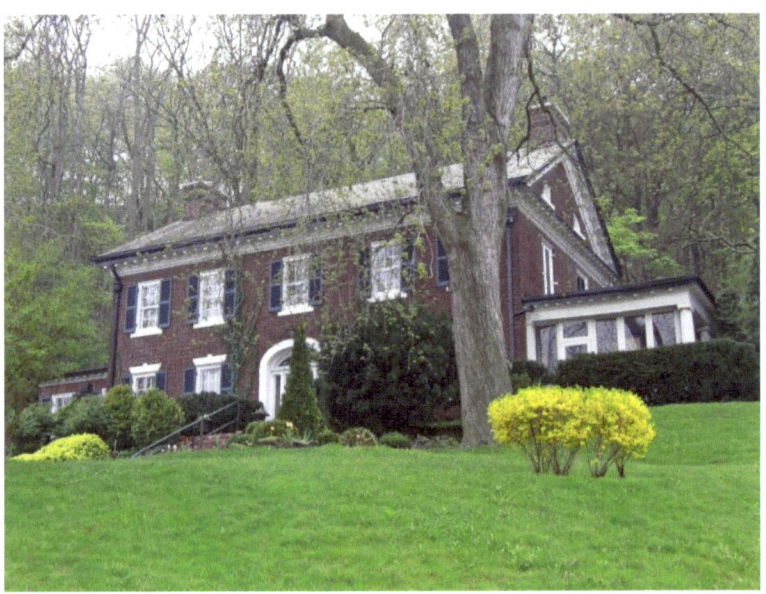

Inglewood Drive - Georgian style, cornice brackets, shutters

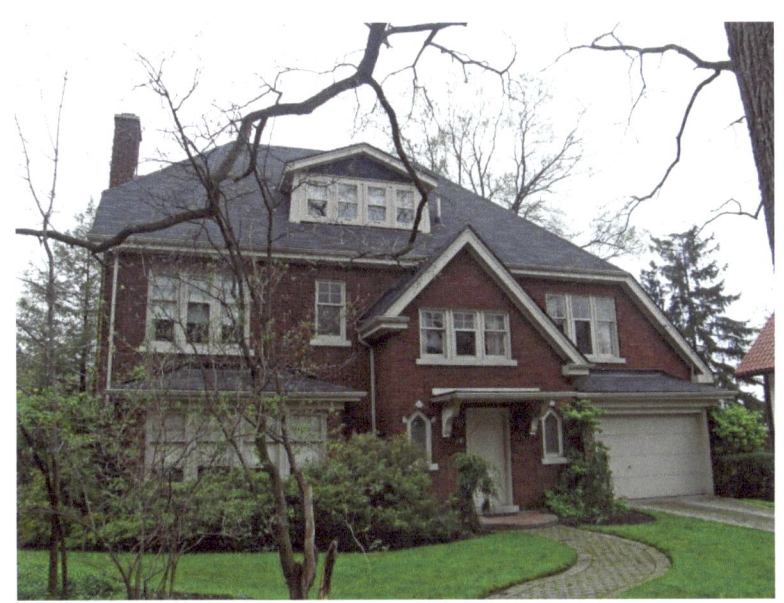

18 Inglewood Drive

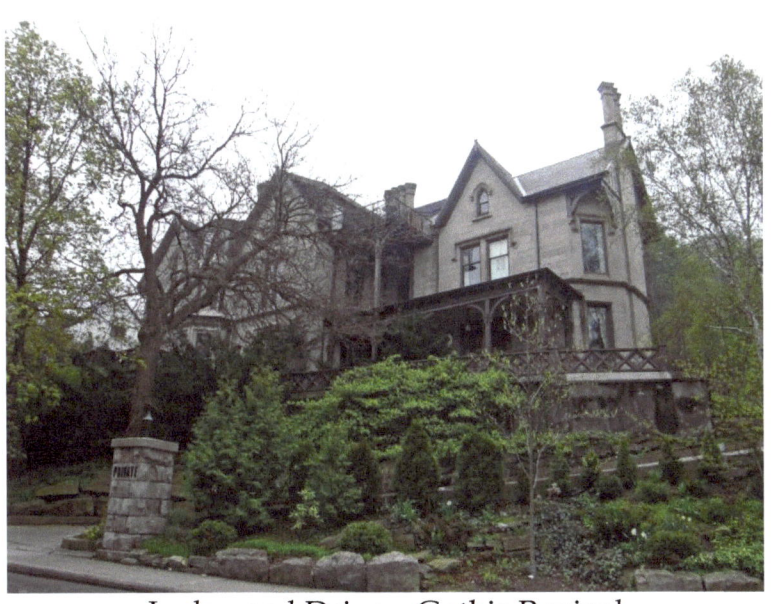

Inglewood Drive – Gothic Revival

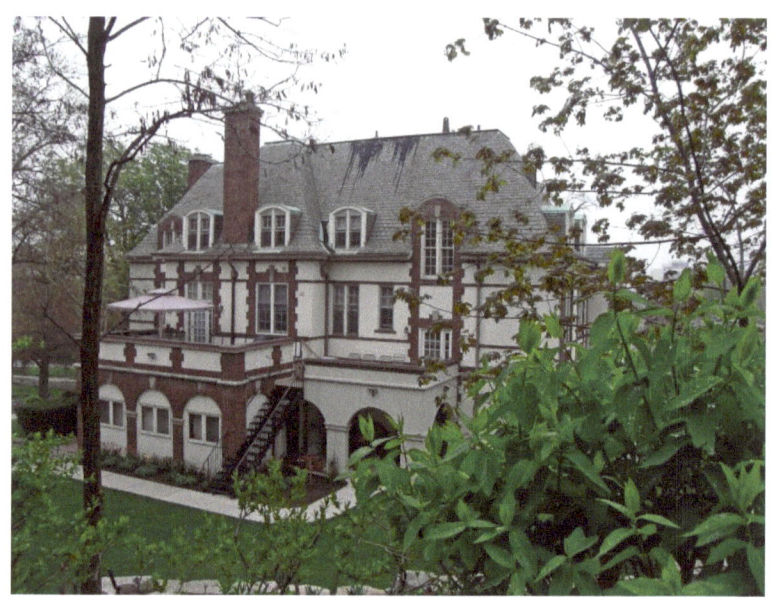

Inglewood Drive - dichromatic brickwork

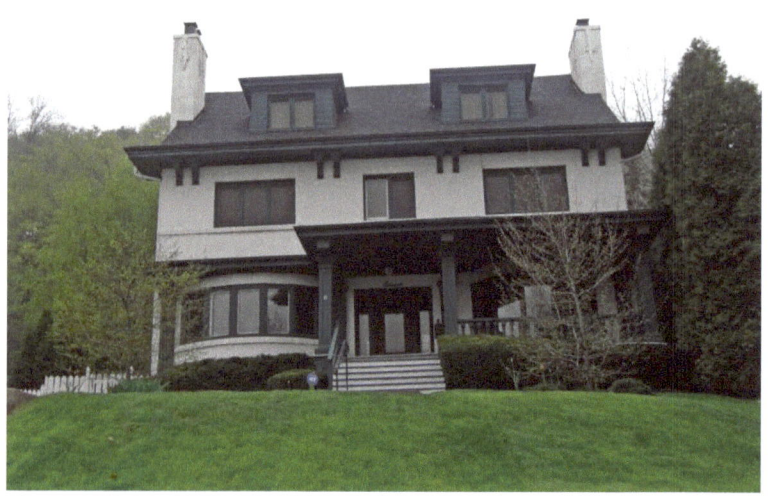

11 Inglewood Drive – Italianate, dormers,
paired cornice brackets

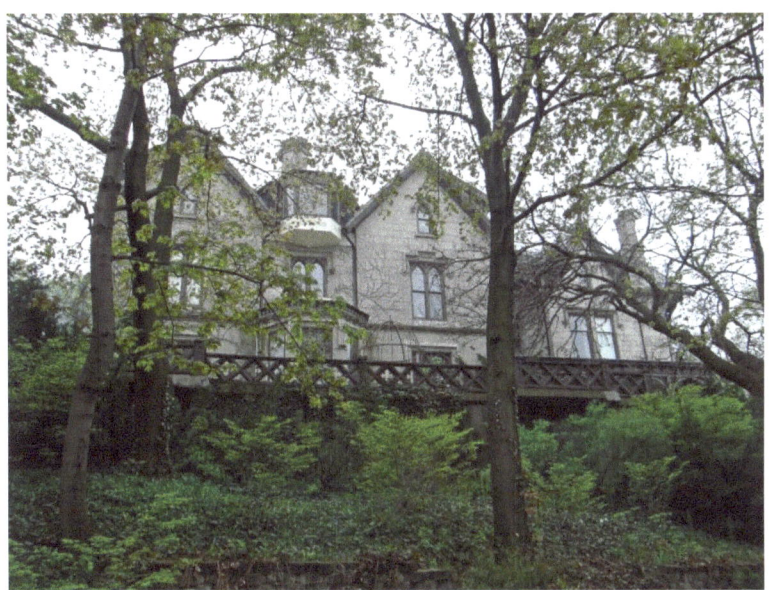

The Inglewood – Tudor Gothic Revival Villa built c. 1850 for Archibald Kerr, a Scotsman in the wholesale dry goods trade. The doors, window panes and fireplaces were enhanced with hand-carved Gothic motifs in the 28-room villa built on 12 acres of land overlooking the city and bay.

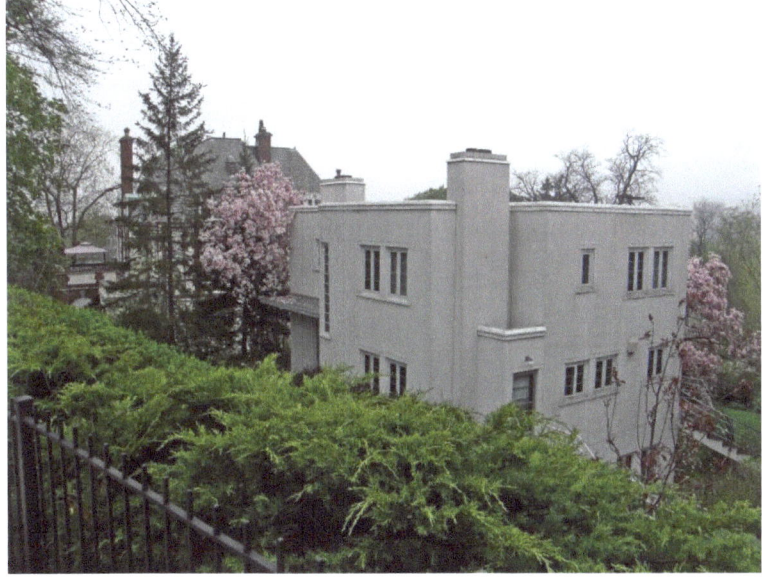

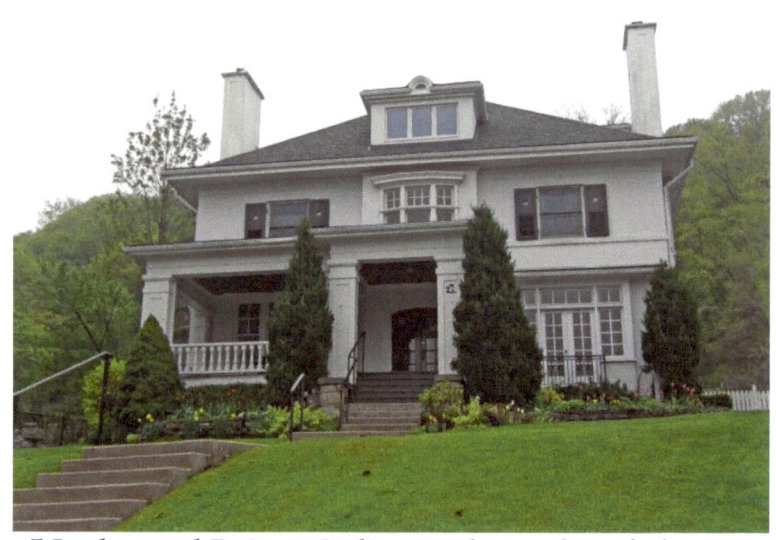

5 Inglewood Drive – Italianate, hipped roof, dormer

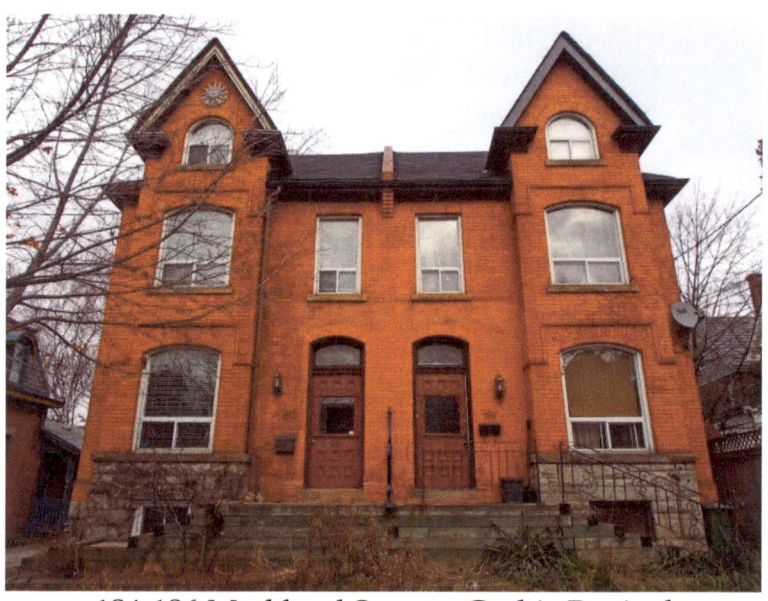

184-186 Markland Street – Gothic Revival

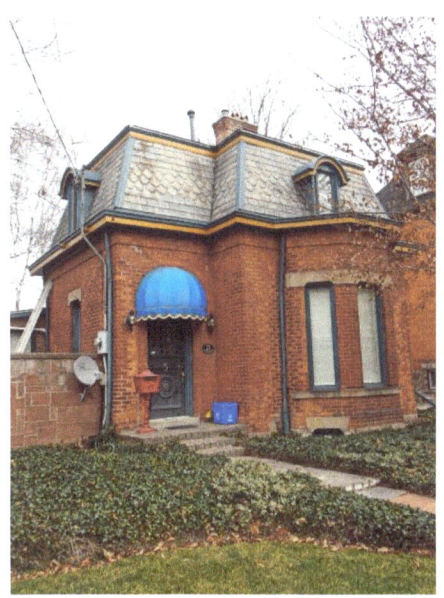

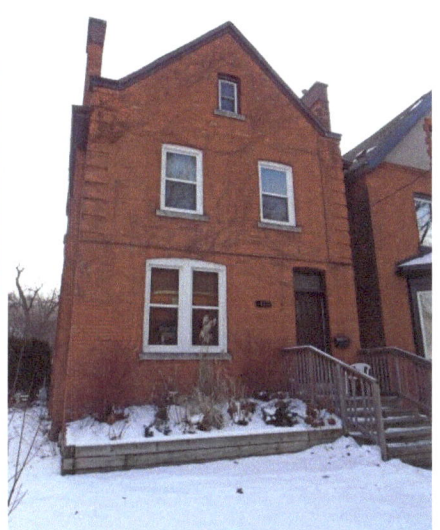

188 Markland Street c. 1895
Second Empire, mansard roof
Queen Street Pump House
residence

177 Markland Street

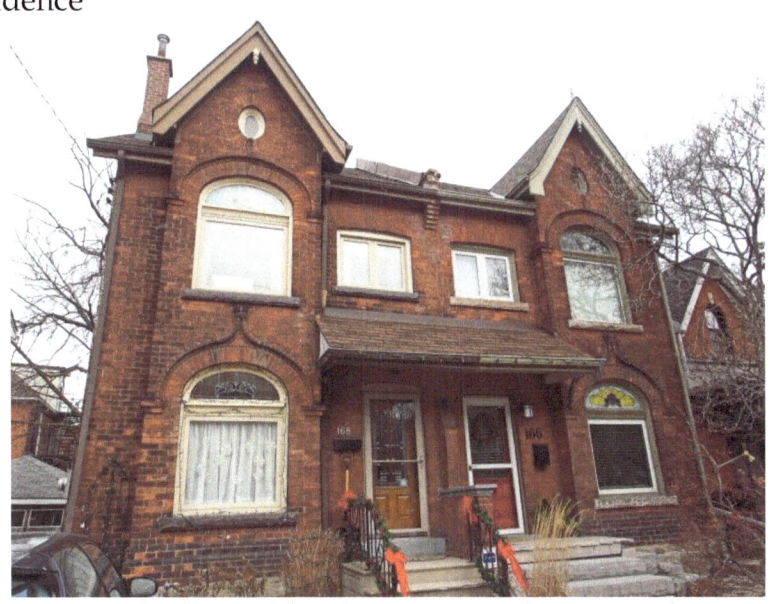

166-168 Markland Street – Gothic Revival

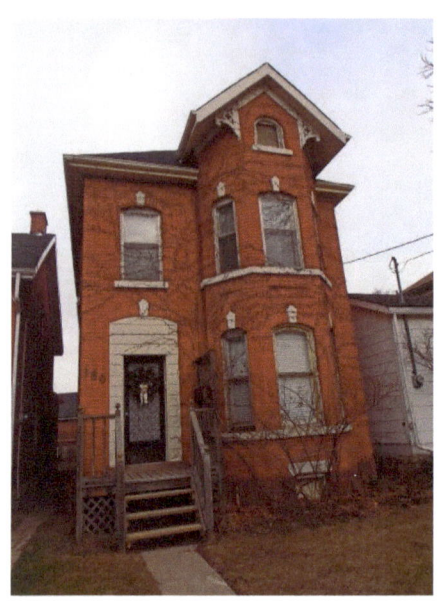

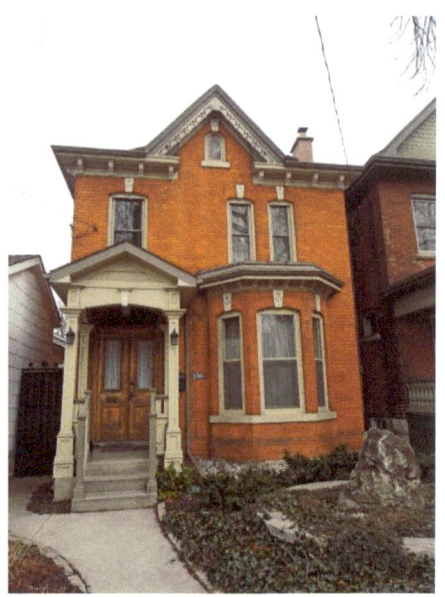

160 Markland Street
fretwork
2½-storey bay window

156 Markland Street
Pediment, bay window
Cornice brackets

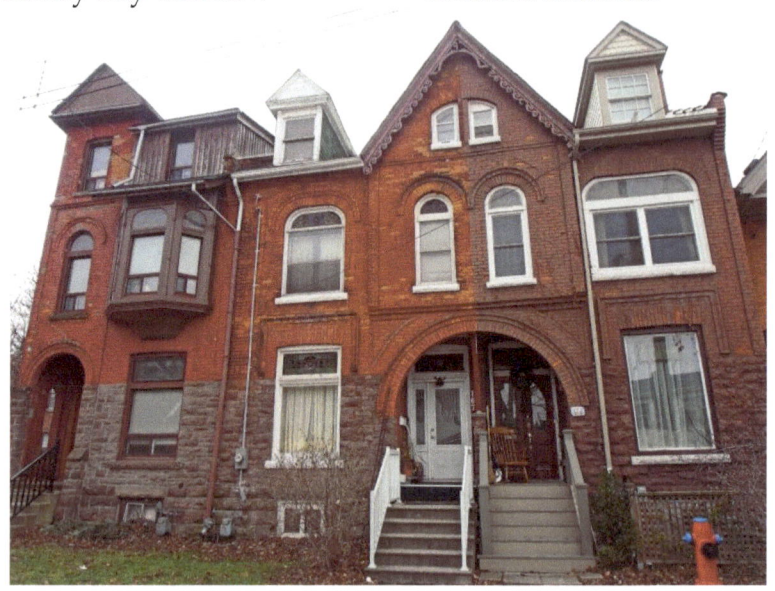

165-169 Markland Street – Gothic Revival,
verge board trim on gable, dormers

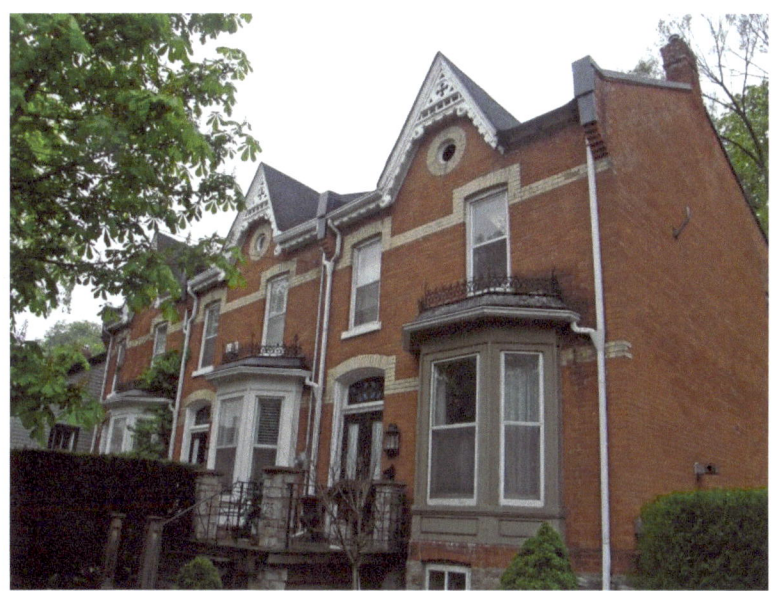

147-149 Markland Street – Gothic Revival, verge board trim, iron cresting above bay windows, banding

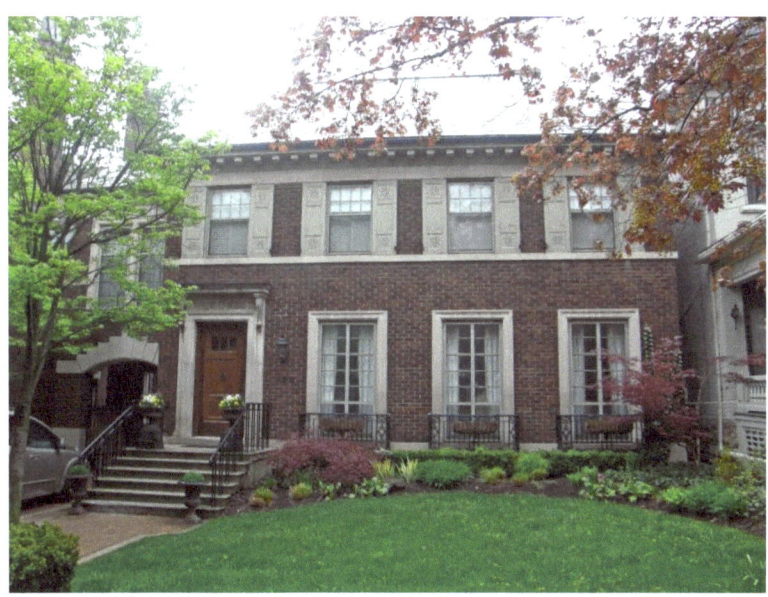

#120 Markland Street – Georgian/Neo-Classical style with intricate patterning on the sides of the upper windows

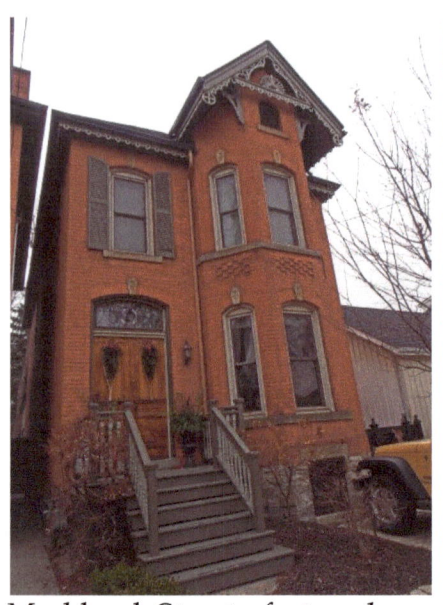

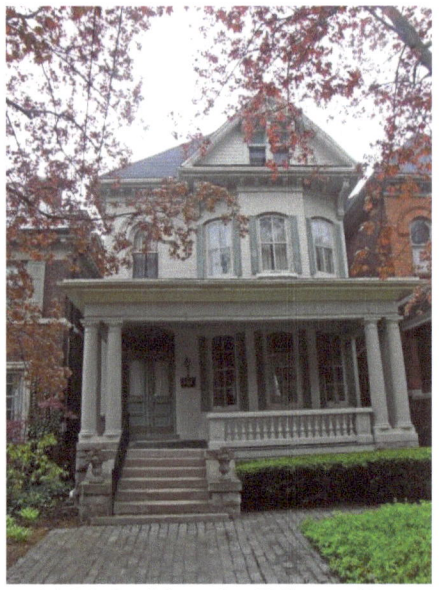

Markland Street - fretwork verge board trim on gable 2½ storey tower-like bay

118 Markland - Edwardian

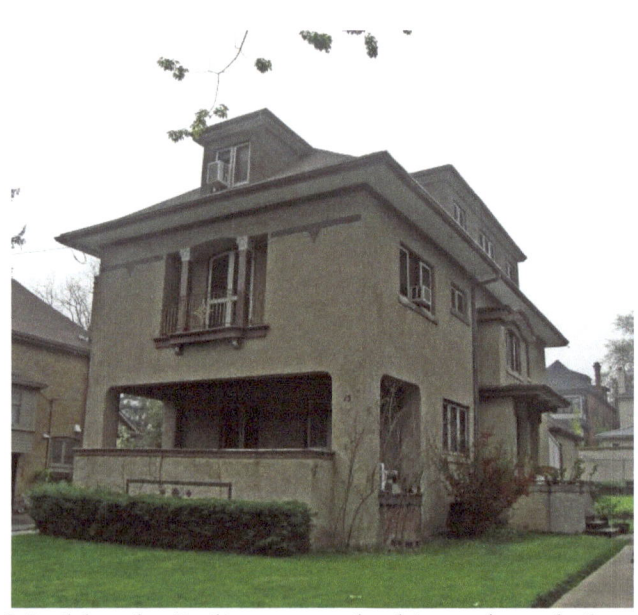

115 Markland – Italianate style, hipped roof, dormers

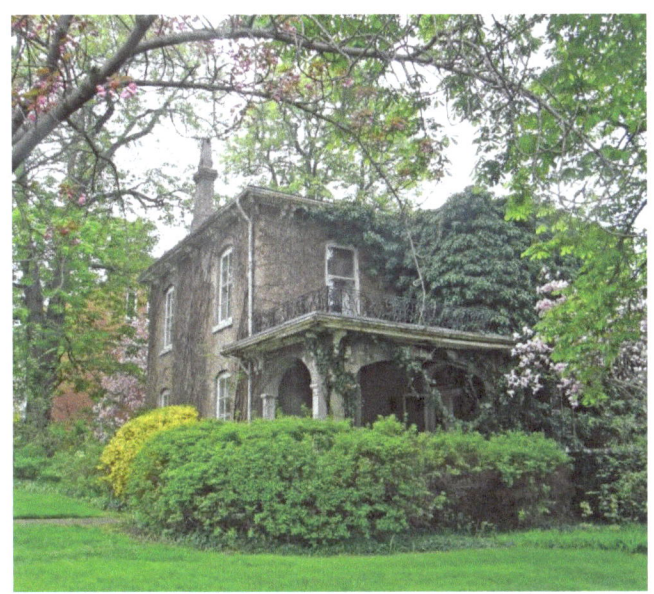

Italianate, verandah on second floor

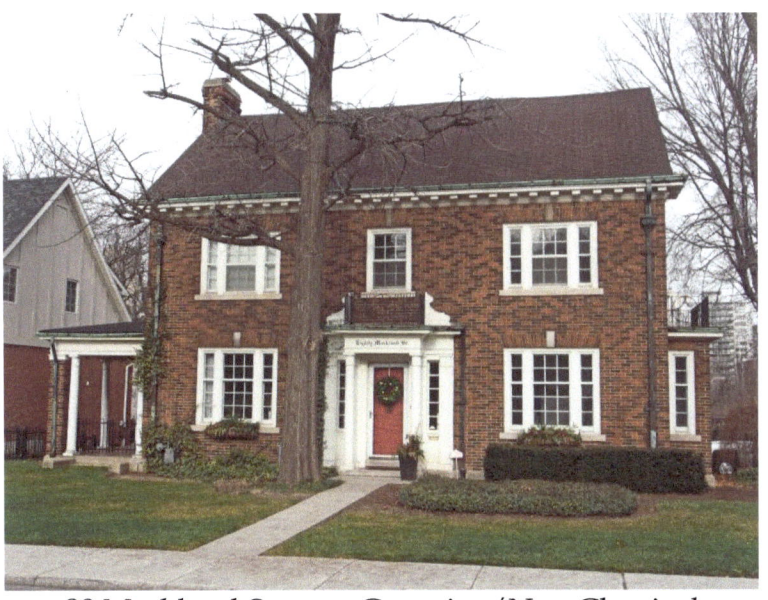

80 Markland Street – Georgian/Neo-Classical

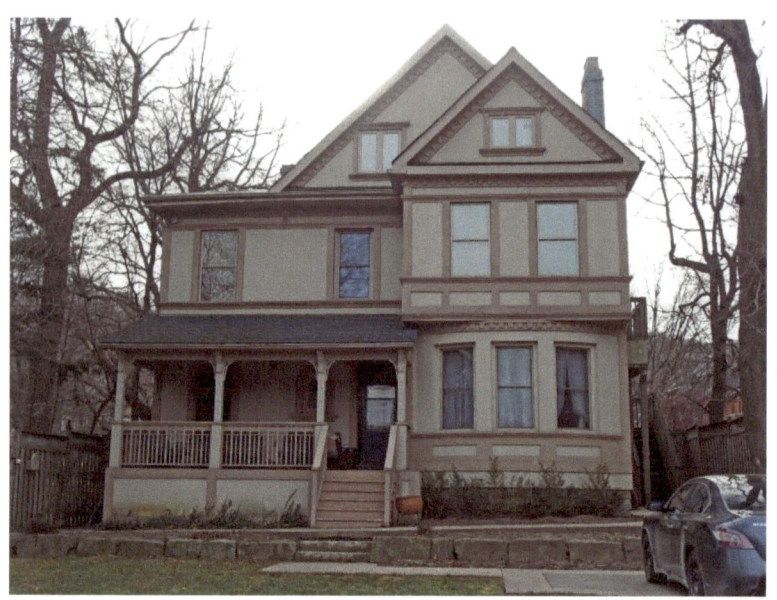

79 Markland Street

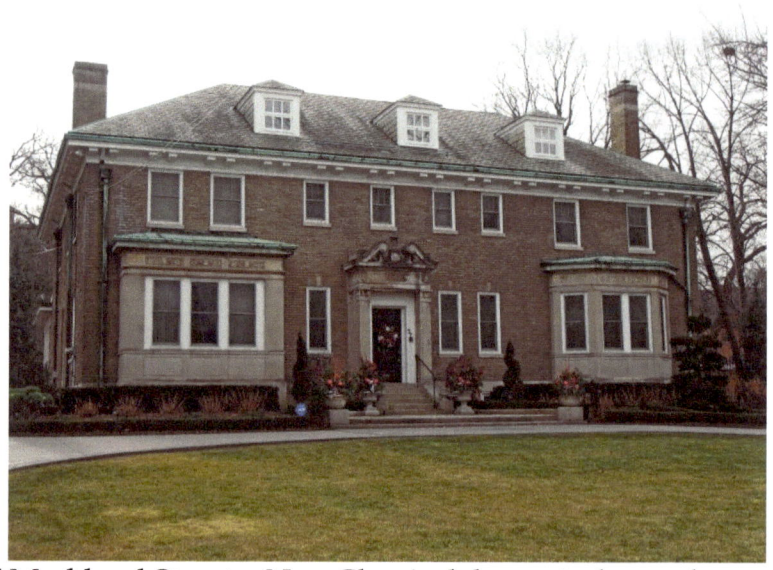

77 Markland Street – Neo-Classical, bay windows, dormers

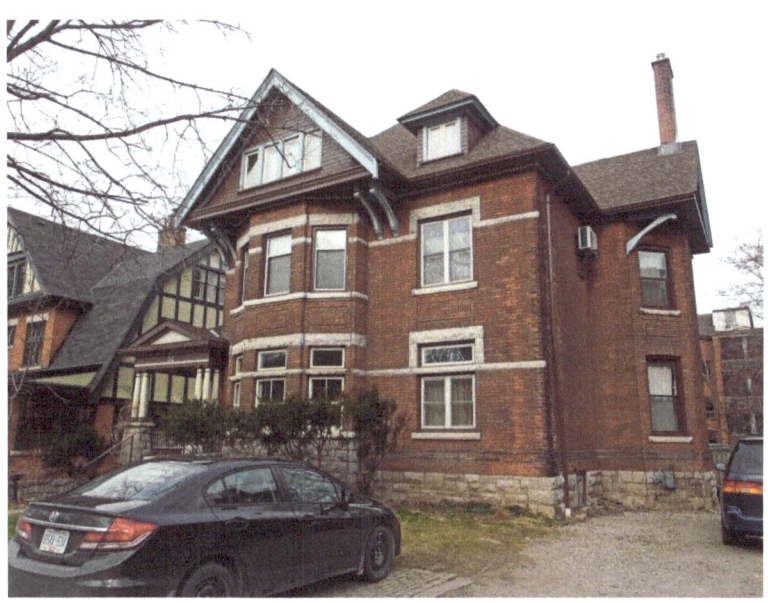

52 Markland Street – Edwardian

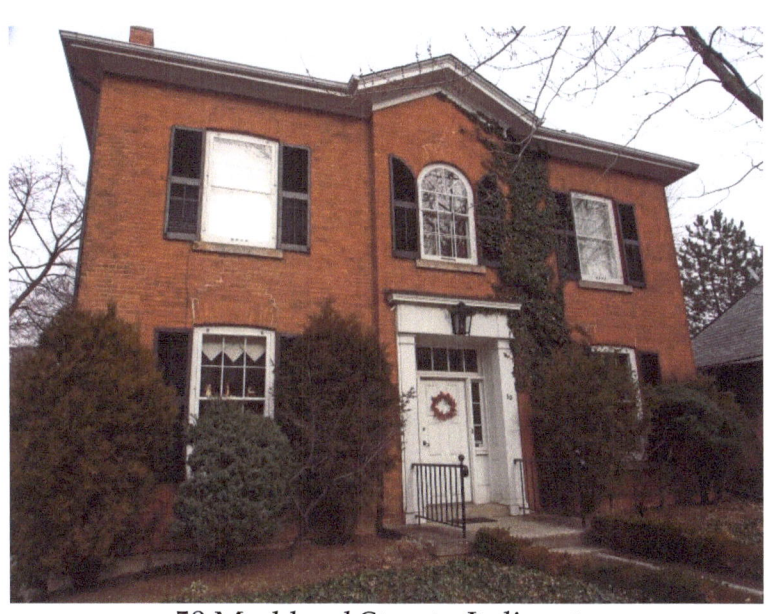

50 Markland Street - Italianate

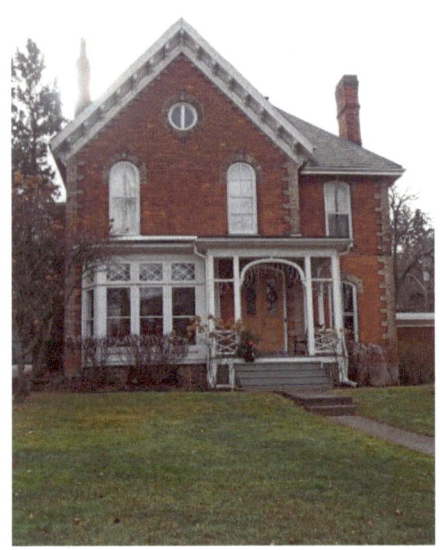

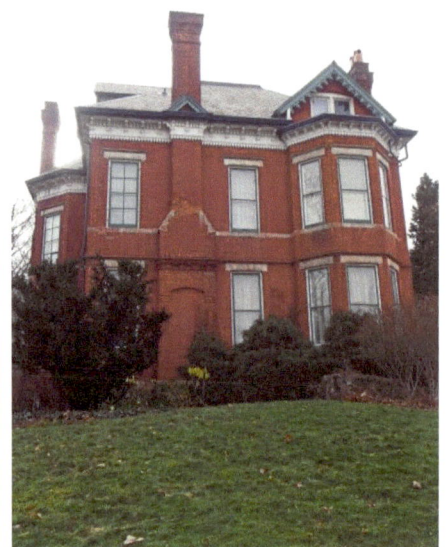

Markland Street
Gothic Revival
cornice brackets

Markland Street
2½-storey bay window
banding

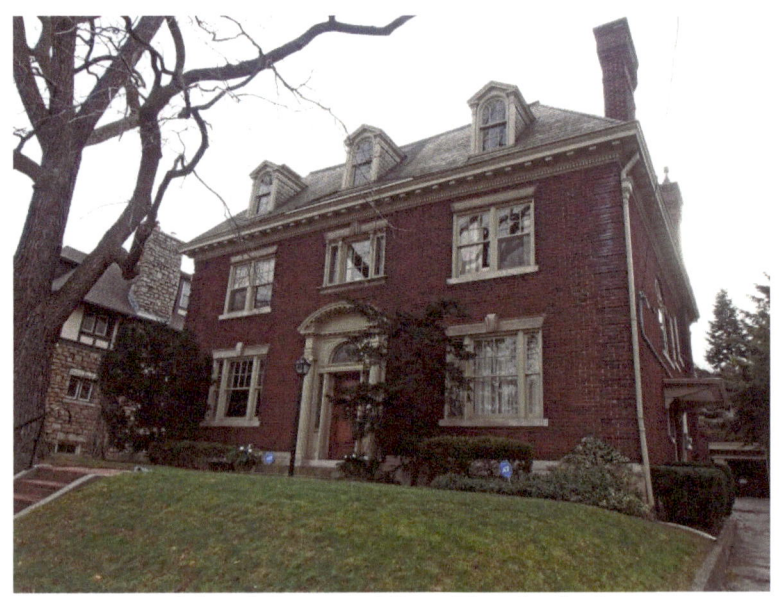

45 Markland Street – Neo-Classical, dormers

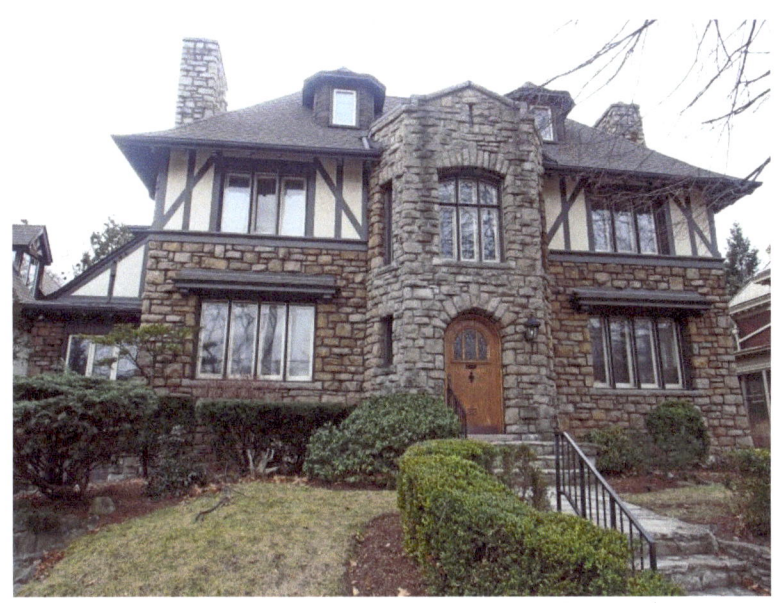

33 Markland Street – stone – Tudor style

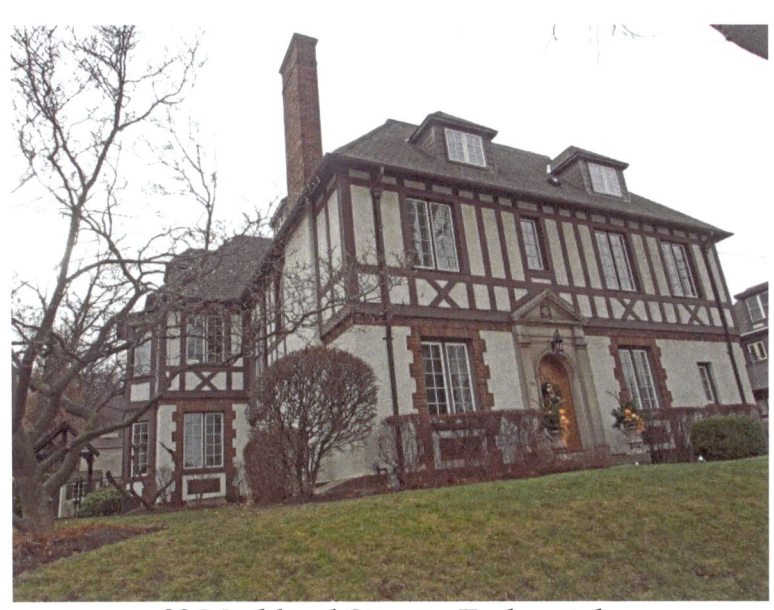

29 Markland Street – Tudor style

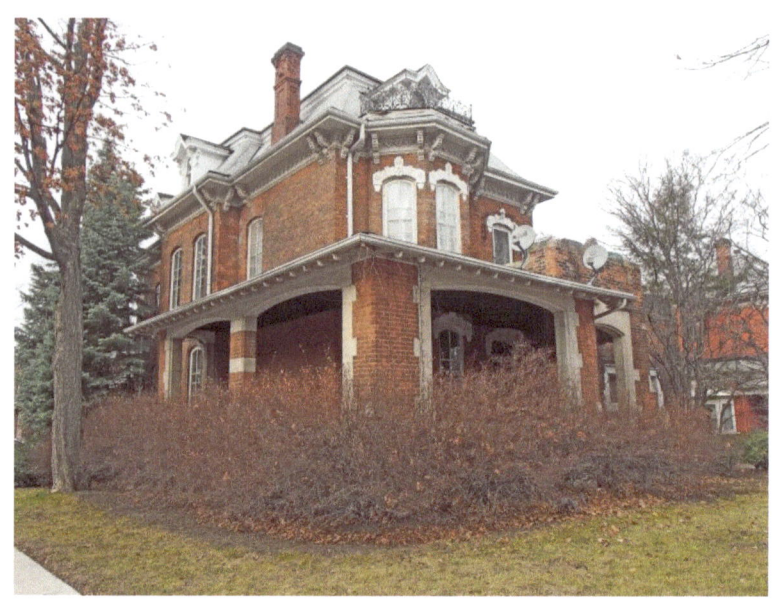

Markland Street – Second Empire, mansard roof, iron cresting, bay window, cornice brackets

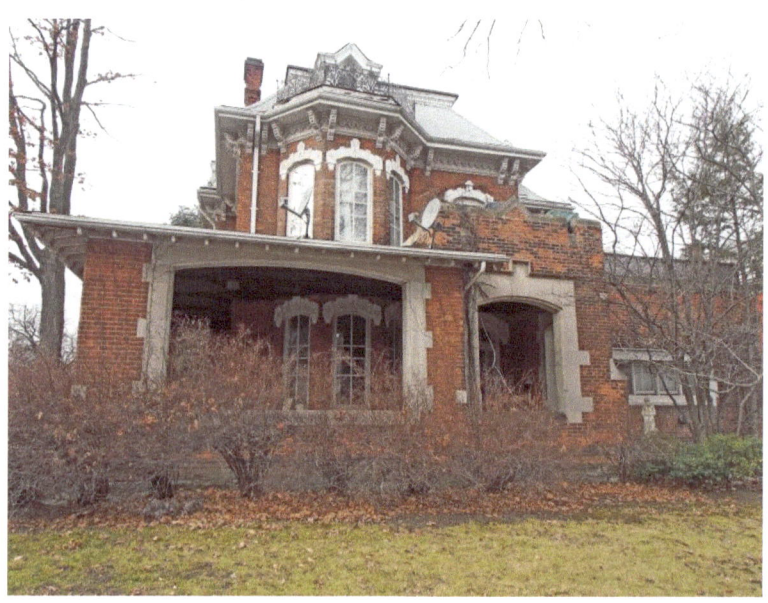

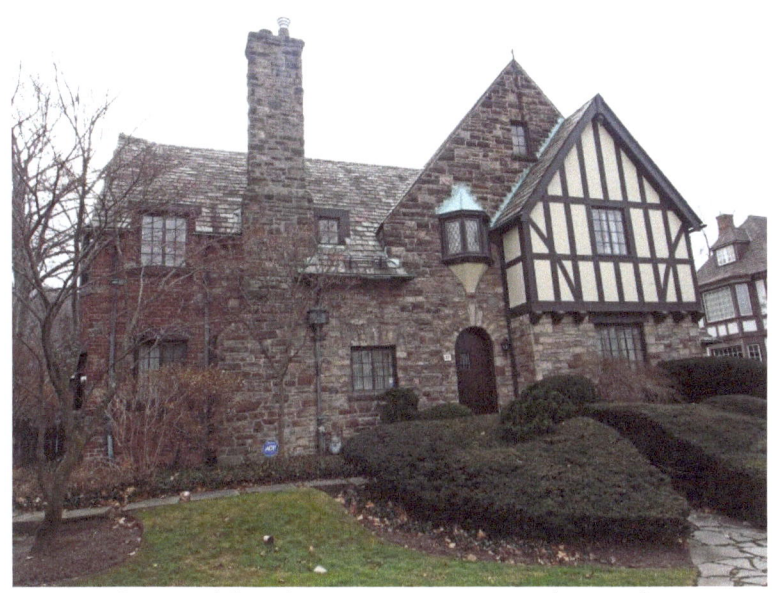

21 Markland Street – stone, Tudor style

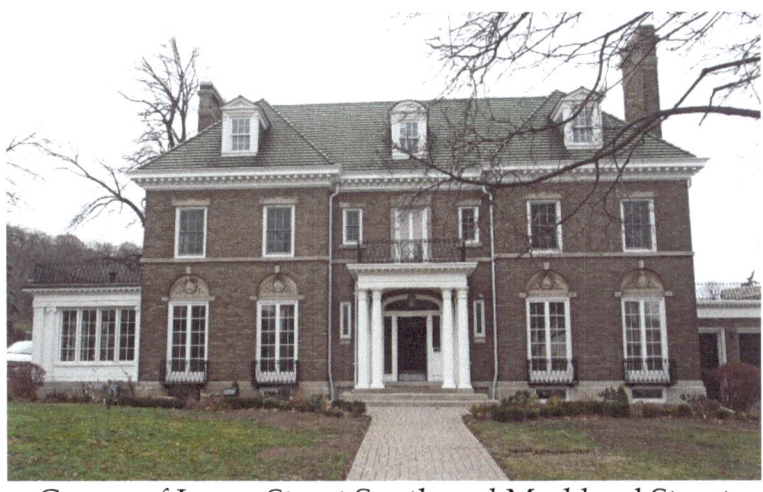

Corner of James Street South and Markland Street
Neo-Classical style, dormers, decorative cement work below
the arched window voussoirs with keystones, dentil moulding
below cornice, dormers in attic

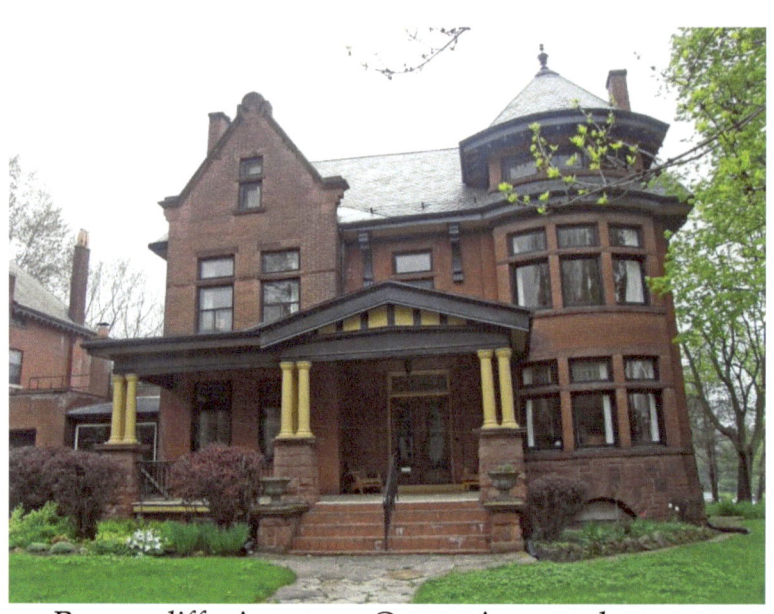

Ravenscliffe Avenue – Queen Anne style, turret

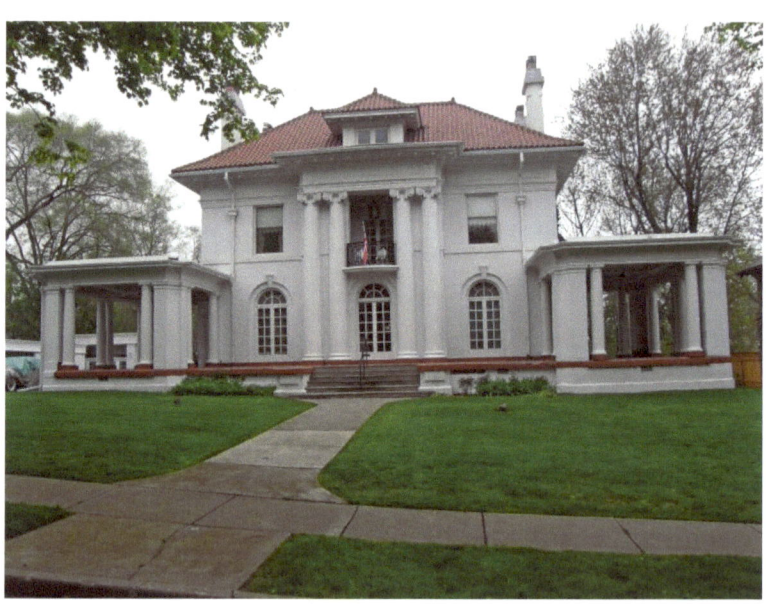

Ravenscliffe Avenue - Italianate style, Ionic capitals on two-storey pillars, dormer in attic, verandah on each side of house

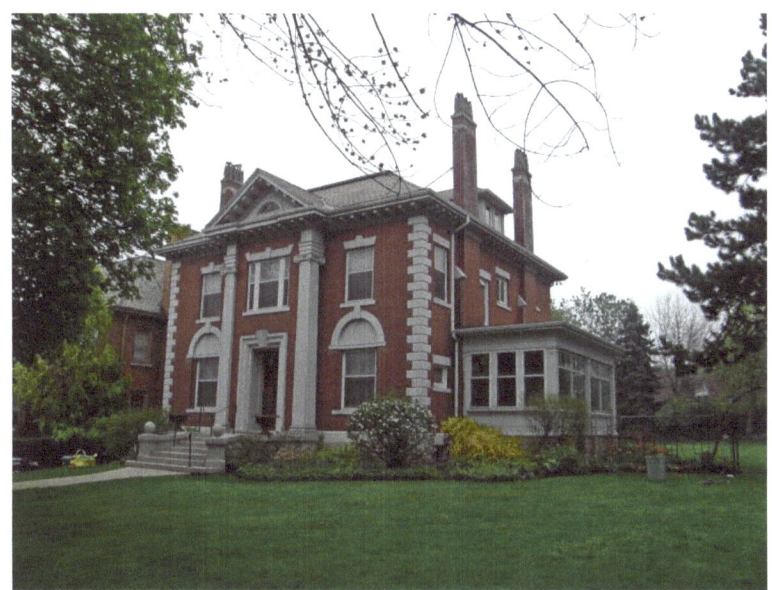

Ravenscliffe Avenue – Italianate, pediment, corner quoins,
Ionic capitals on two-storey pillars, keystones

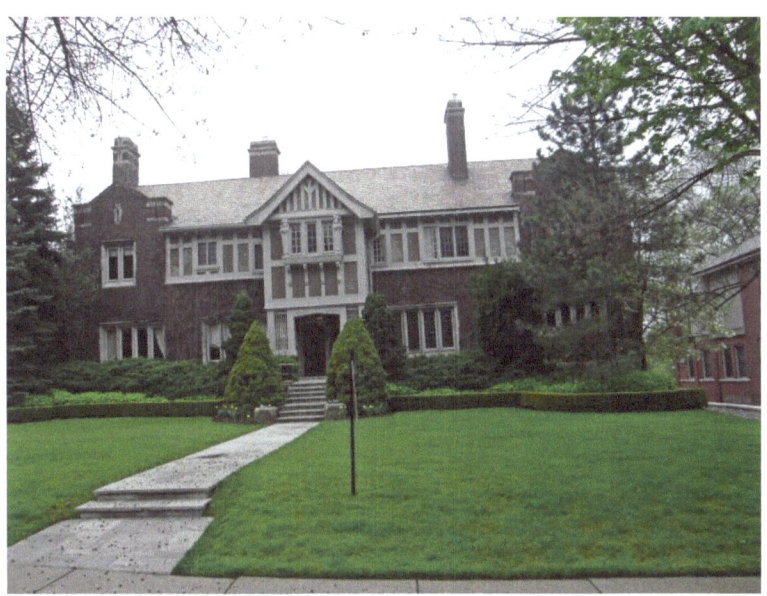

Ravenscliffe Avenue – Tudor style

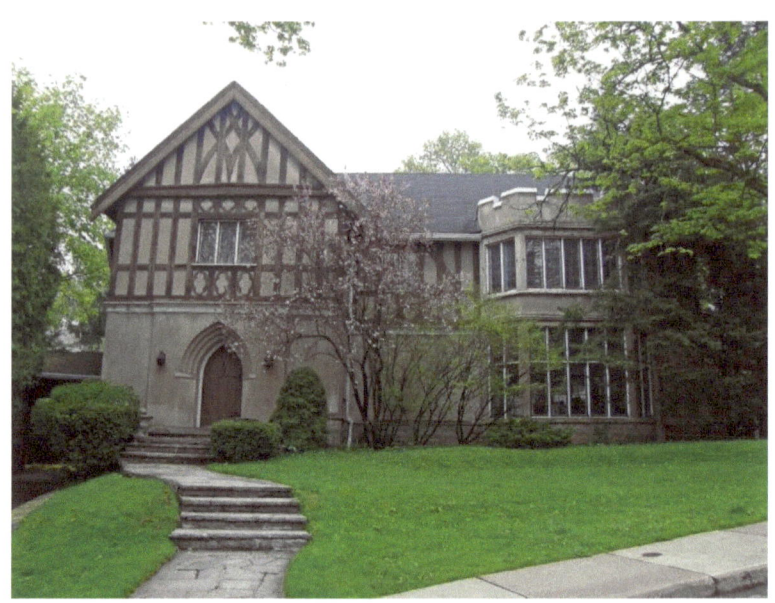

15 Ravenscliffe Avenue – Tudor style

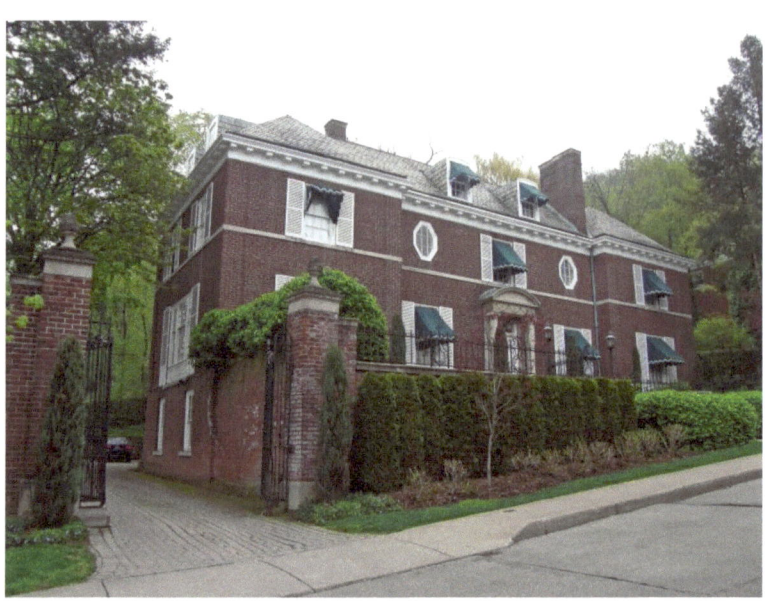

Ravenscliffe Avenue – Italianate style, dormers in attic

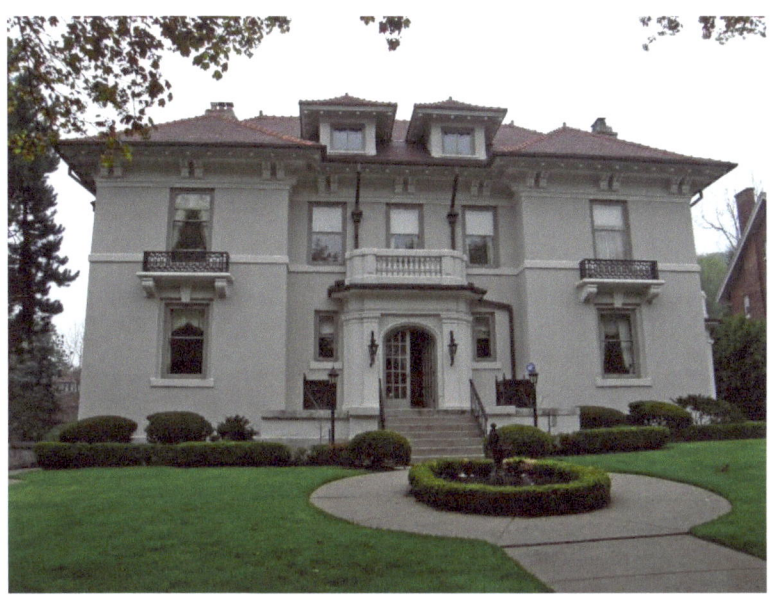

7 Ravenscliffe Avenue – built in 1910 - designed for Henry B. Witton, Vice President of the Tuckett Tobacco Company, by his brother, William Palmer Witton, a well-regarded Hamilton architect who also designed the Herkimer Apartments and many homes in the Durand neighbourhood.

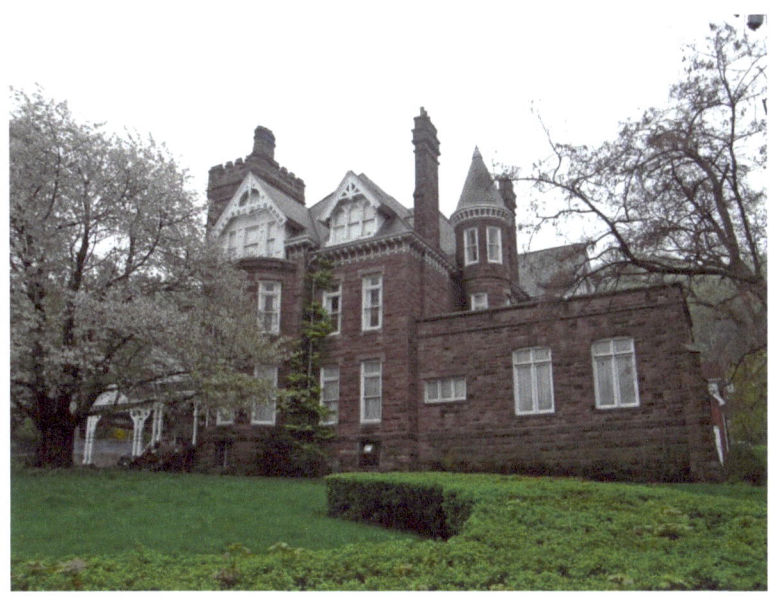

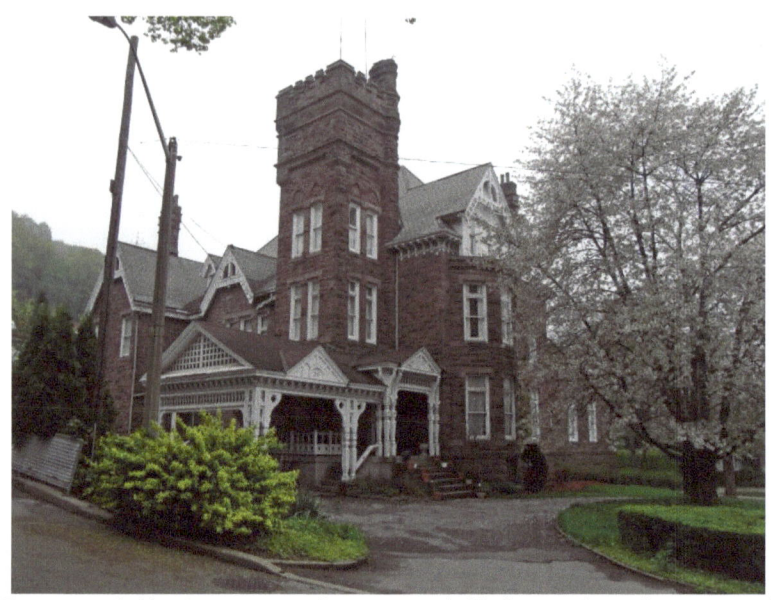

Ravenscliffe Avenue - "Ravenscliffe" – palatial estate of wealthy industrialist William Copp – built by James Balfour – stone, Queen Anne style

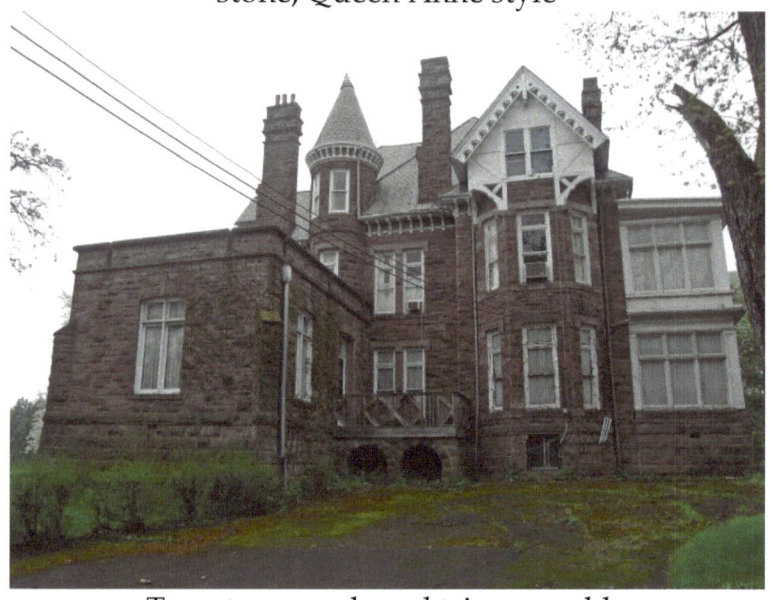

Turrets, verge board trim on gable

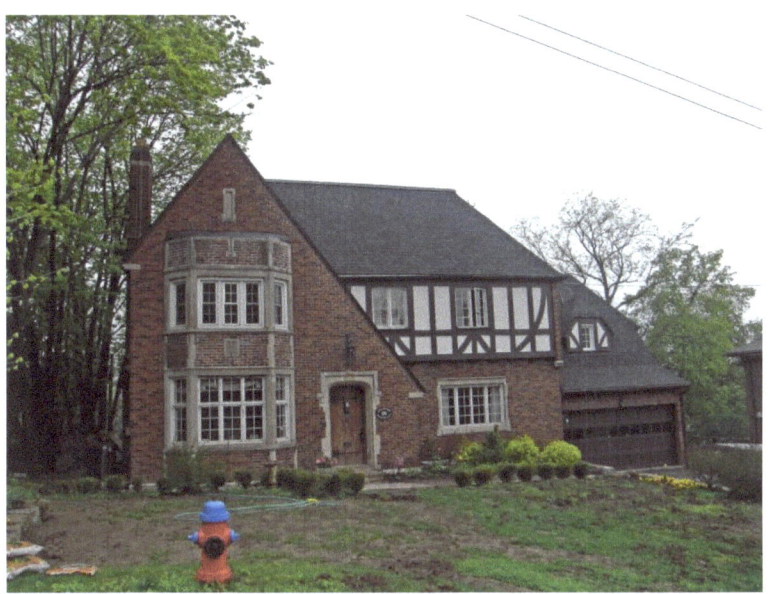

20 Ravenscliffe Avenue – "Highview" – Tudor style

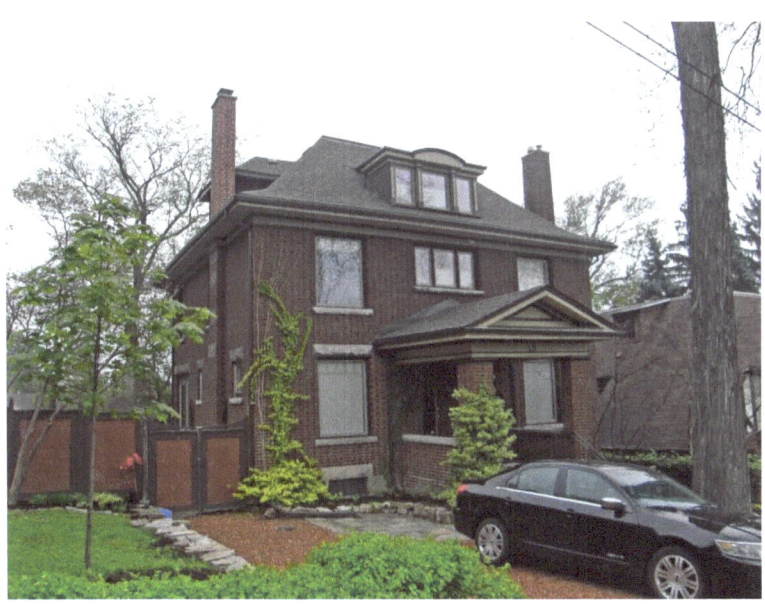

Ravenscliffe Avenue – Italianate, dormers, pediment

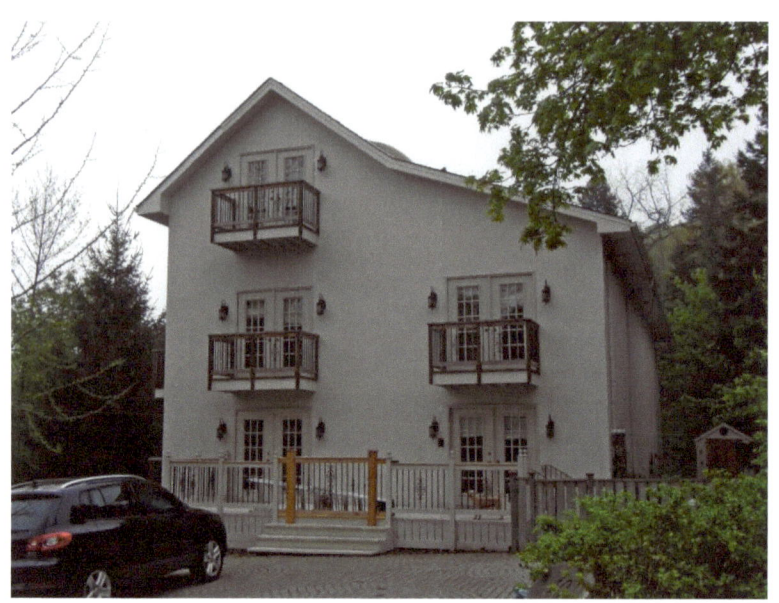

Ravenscliffe Avenue

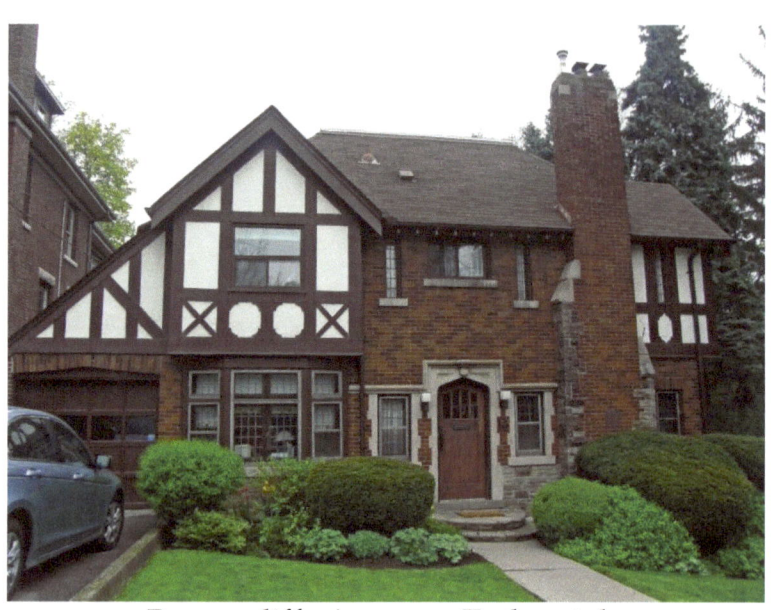

Ravenscliffe Avenue - Tudor style

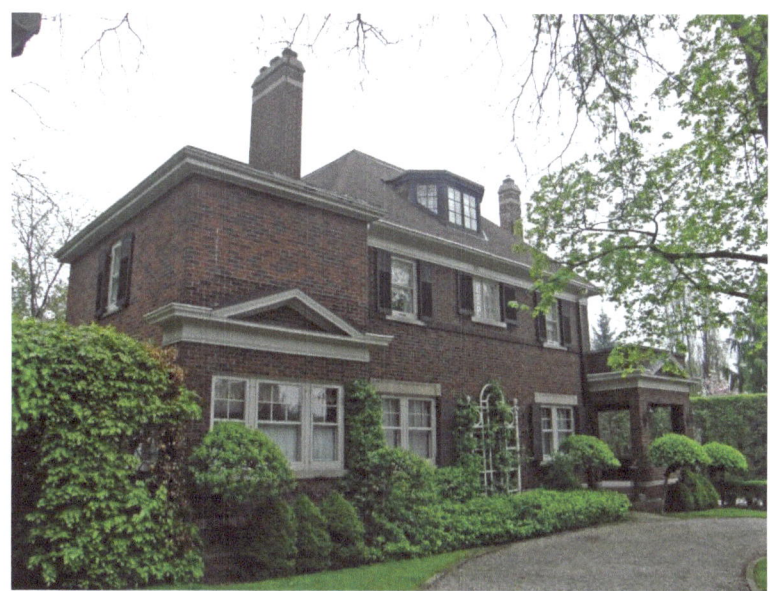

Ravenscliffe Avenue – Italianate, dormer, pediment

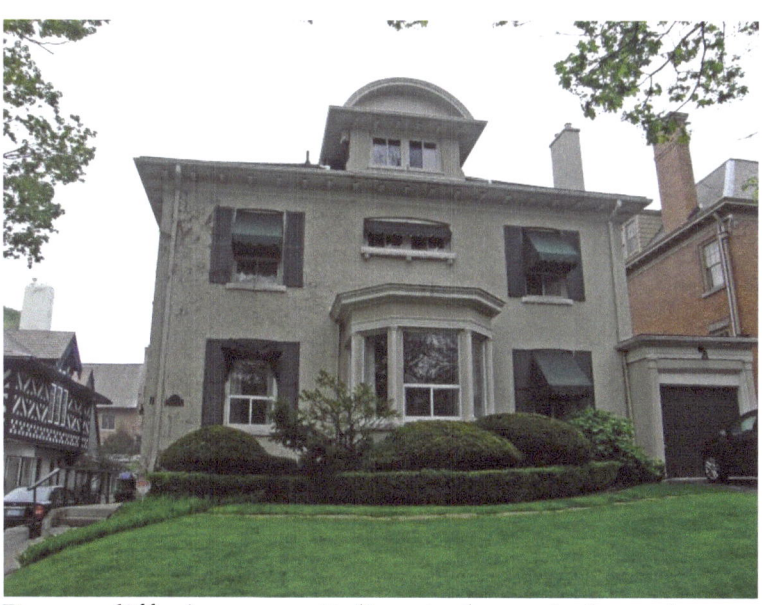

Ravenscliffe Avenue – Italianate, bay window, dormer

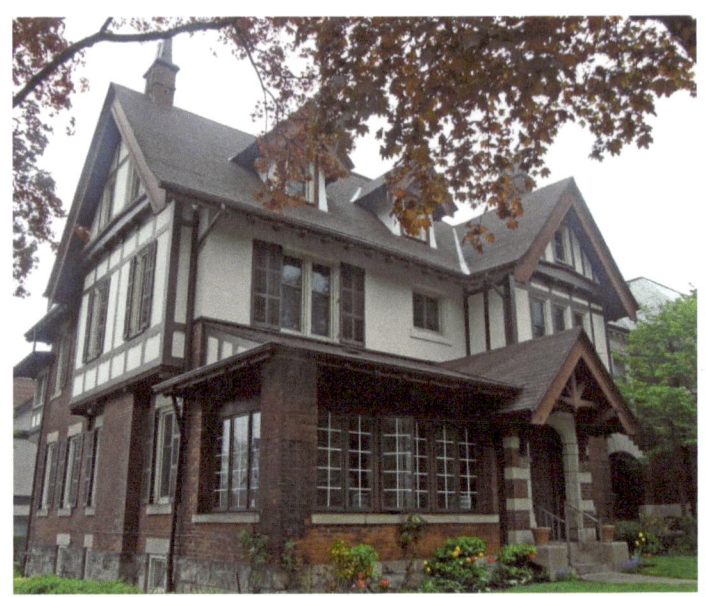

Ravenscliffe Avenue – Tudor style

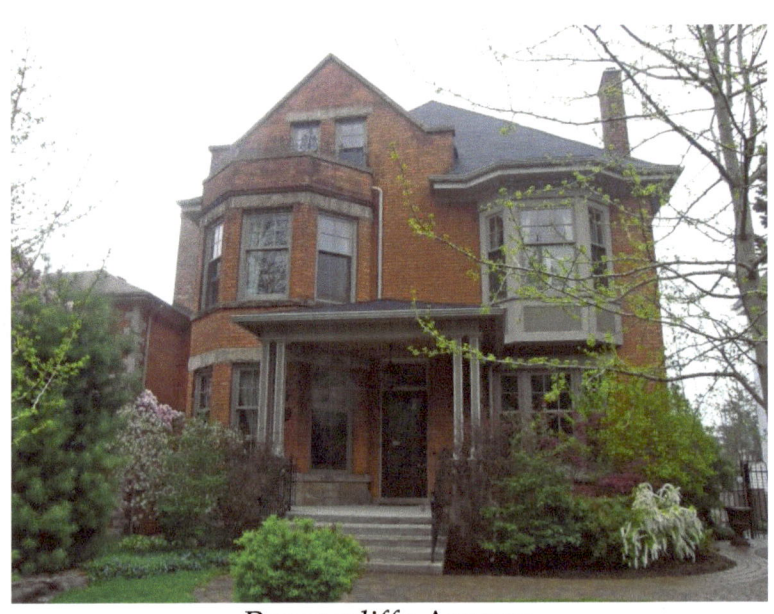

Ravenscliffe Avenue

Architectural Terms

Brackets: a decorative or weight-bearing structural element which forms a right angle with one side against a wall and the other under a projecting surface such as an eave or roof. Example: Markland Street (see Page 42)	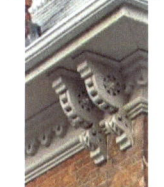
Capital: The uppermost finish or decoration on a column. An Ionic column has a small base, a thin elegant shaft, and a capital composed of volutes which are carved whirls or twists that take the form of a scroll. Example: 351-353 Bay Street South	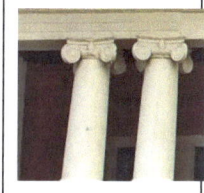
Cornice: originally the wooden overhang of the roof. With the use of stone, brick, iron and steel, the cornice is any projecting shelf at the top of a ceiling or roof. They can be very decorative. Example: Markland Street (see Page 42)	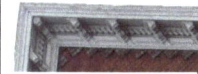
Dentil Moulding: an even series of rectangles used as ornamental decoration in cornices. Example: 357 Bay Street South	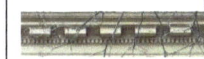
Dichromatic brickwork: the use of two colours of brick, tile or slate to decorate a façade. Example: Inglewood Drive (see Page 32)	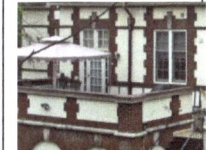
Dormer: (French for "sleep") a gable end window that pierces through the plane of a sloping roof surface to create usable space in the top floor or attic of a building by adding headroom. Example: 126 Aberdeen Avenue	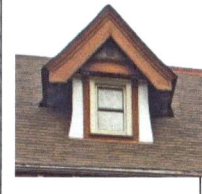

Fretwork: interlaced decorative design resembling a bracket Example: Aberdeen Avenue (see Page 10)	
Gable: the triangular portion of a wall between the edges of a sloping roof. Example: 167-169 Markland Street	
Hipped Roof: a roof where all sides slope downwards to the walls with no gables. Example: corner of James Street South and Markland Street (see Page 45)	
Iron Cresting: A decorative ornament along the top of a roof. Iron cresting was popular in the Baroque era and also in Italianate, Victorian, Second Empire and Queen Anne styles of architecture. 269 Bay Street South	
Keystones and Voussoirs: a voussoir is a wedge-shaped element used in building an arch. A keystone is the central stone that locks all the stones into position, allowing the arch to bear weight. A keystone is often enlarged and embellished. Example: corner James Street South and Markland Streets	

Mansard Roof: This style was popularized by Francois Mansart (1598-1666), an accomplished architect of the French Baroque period and especially fashionable during the Second French Empire (1852-1870). This roof is almost flat on the top section, with two slopes on each of its sides with the lower slope at a steeper angle than the upper and having dormer windows. Example: 188 Markland Street	
Palladian Window: a large window that is divided into three sections with the centre section larger than the two side sections and usually arched. Example: 353 Bay Street South	
Pediment: a triangular section above the horizontal structure (entablature), typically supported by columns. The inside of the triangle is called the tympanum. Example: 282 Bay Street South	
Quoin: masonry blocks at the corner of a wall, often a decorative feature, usually larger or of a different colour than the rest of the wall. Example: Ravenscliffe Avenue (see Page 47)	

Turret: a small tower that projects from the wall of a building. Example: Ravenscliffe Manor	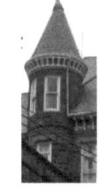
Verge board and Finial: also called bargeboards – hang from the projecting end of a roof and are often elaborately carved and ornamented. **Finial:** ornament added to the top of a gable, pinnacle, canopy or spire – a Gothic element. Example: Ravenscliffe Manor	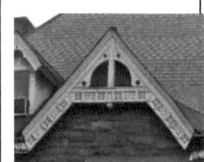

Building Styles

Edwardian, 1900-1930 – This style bridges the ornate and elaborate styles of the Victorian era and the simplified styles of the 20th century. Balanced facades, simple roof lines, dormer windows, large front porches, and smooth brick surfaces are its characteristics. Example: 327 Bay Street South	
Georgian, before 1860 – This style began with the British King Georges in the 18th century. These buildings have balanced facades around a central door, medium-pitched gable roofs, and small paned windows. Example: 43 Inglewood Drive	
Gothic Revival, 1830-1890 – These decorative buildings have sharply-pitched gables with highly detailed verge boards, pointed-arch window openings, and dichromatic brickwork. It is a common style in Ontario. Example: 64 Aberdeen Avenue	
Italianate, 1850-1900 – It has wide-bracketed eaves, belvederes, wrap-around verandahs. Example: 312 Bay Street South	

Neo-Classical (1810 - 1850) – This style was a direct result of the War of 1812. Many Upper Canadians returning from the war with the United States were second or third generation Loyalists who had inherited land and means from their forefathers. Once the conflict had passed, they had the money and the time to expand their holdings and indulge their architectural whims. Both residential and commercial buildings were constructed on the traditional Georgian plan, but they had a new gaiety and light-heartedness. Detailing became more refined, delicate, and elegant. Example: 51 Aberdeen Avenue	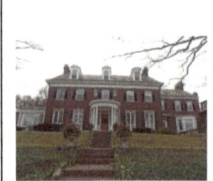
Queen Anne, 1885-1900 – This style is distinguished by an irregular outline featuring a combination of an offset tower, broad gables, projecting two-storey bays, verandahs, multi-sloped roofs, and tall, decorative chimneys. A mixture of brick and wood is common. Windows often have one large single-paned bottom sash and small panes in the upper sash. Example: 60 Aberdeen Avenue	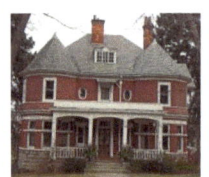
Second Empire, 1860-1880 – The mansard roof is the most noteworthy feature of this style and is evidence of the French origins. Projecting central towers and one or two-storey bays can also be present. Example: 188 Markland Street	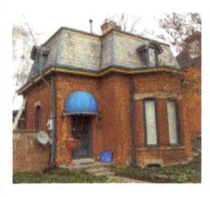